15 Disney VOCAL DUETS
FROM THE STAGE AND SCREEN

for Two Voices and Piano Accompaniment

ISBN 978-1-4803-6900-9

Walt Disney Music Company
Wonderland Music Company, Inc.

DISTRIBUTED BY

HAL•LEONARD®
CORPORATION

7777 W. BLUEMOUND RD. P.O. BOX 13819 MILWAUKEE, WI 53213

In Australia Contact:
Hal Leonard Australia Pty. Ltd.
4 Lentara Court
Cheltenham, Victoria, 3192 Australia
Email: ausadmin@halleonard.com.au

Visit Hal Leonard Online at
www.halleonard.com

CONTENTS

THE BEAUTIFUL BRINY SEA
from Walt Disney's *Bedknobs and Broomsticks*

Words and Music by RICHARD M. SHERMAN
and ROBERT B. SHERMAN

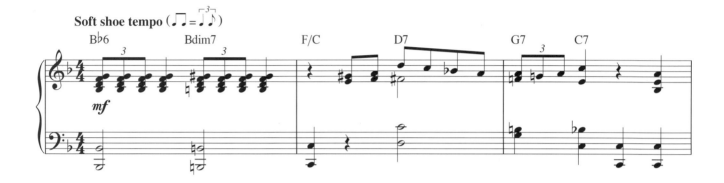

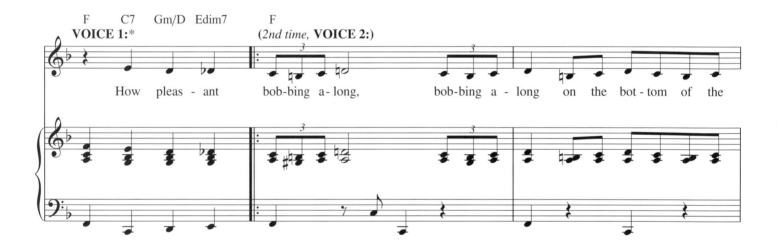

VOICE 1:*
(2nd time, VOICE 2:)

How pleas-ant bob-bing a-long, bob-bing a-long on the bot-tom of the

(2nd time, **BOTH:**)

beau-ti-ful brin — y sea. What a chance to get a bet-ter peep

*A duet for Professor Brown and Miss Price in the film.

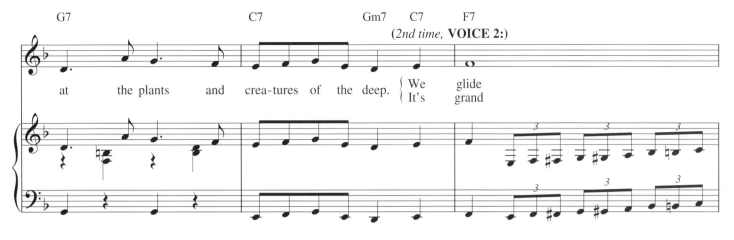

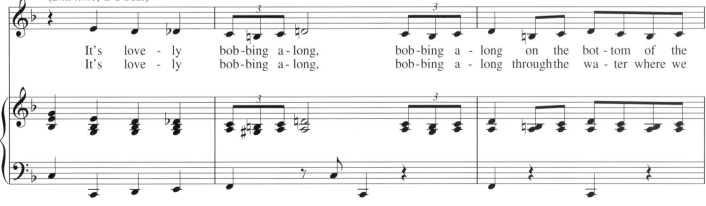

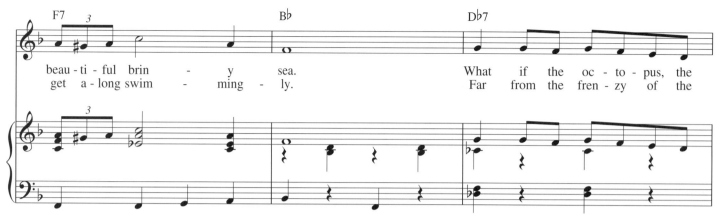

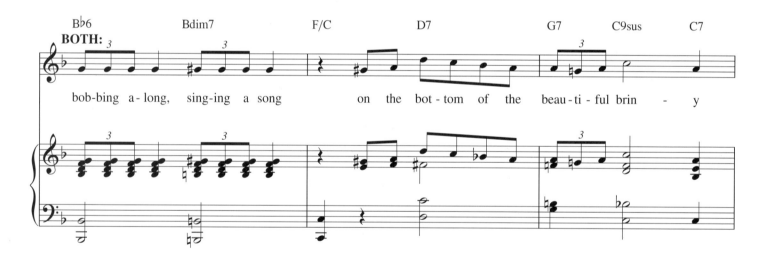

BREAKING FREE
from the Disney Channel Original Movie *High School Musical*

Words and Music by
JAMIE HOUSTON

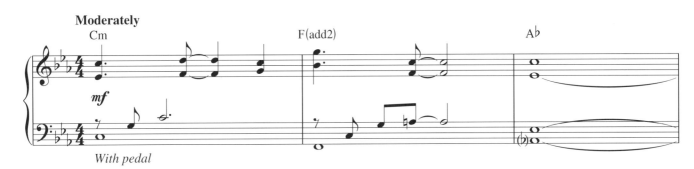

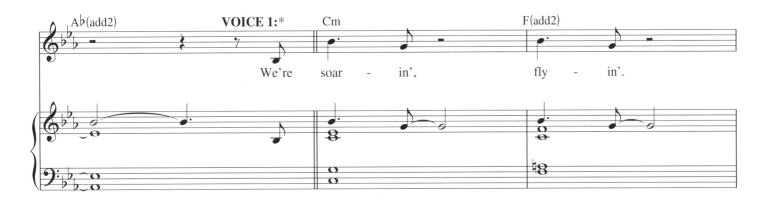

We're soar - in', fly - in'.

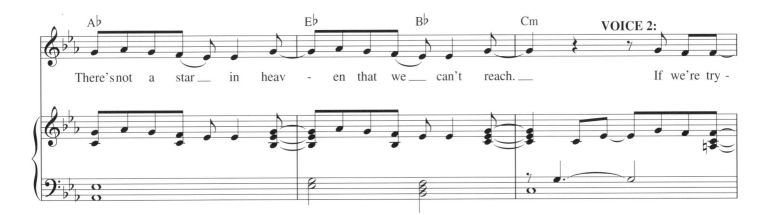

There's not a star in heav - en that we can't reach. If we're try -

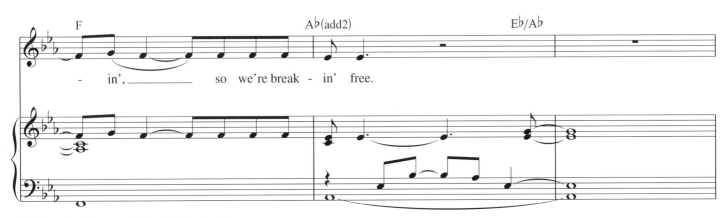

- in', so we're break - in' free.

*A duet for Troy and Gabriella in the film.

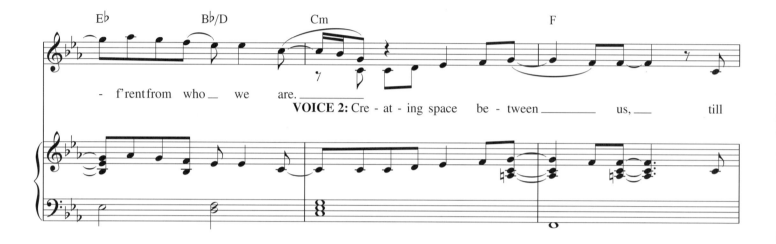

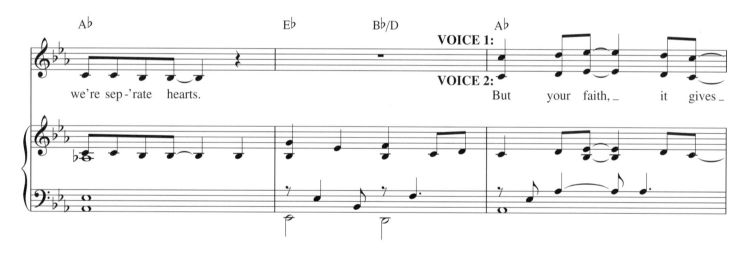

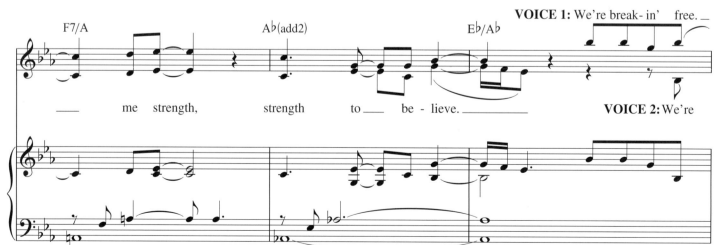

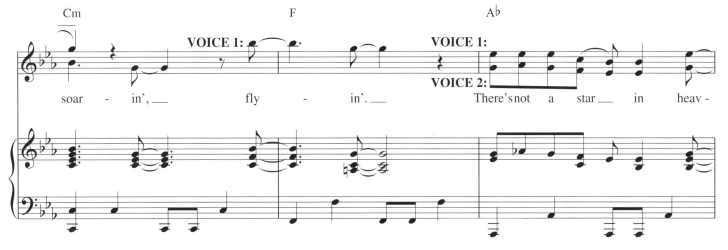

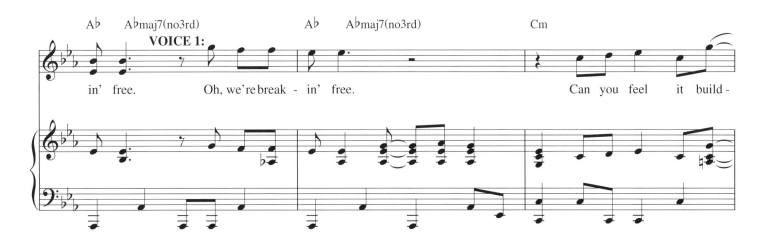

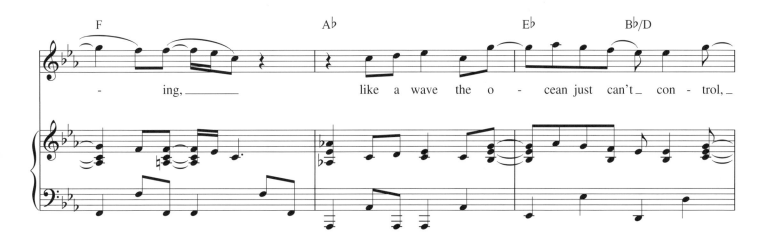

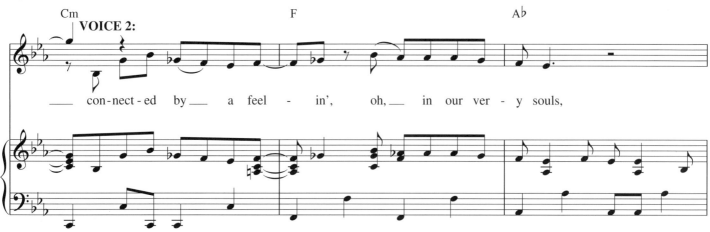

con-nect-ed by __ a feel - in', oh, __ in our ver - y souls,

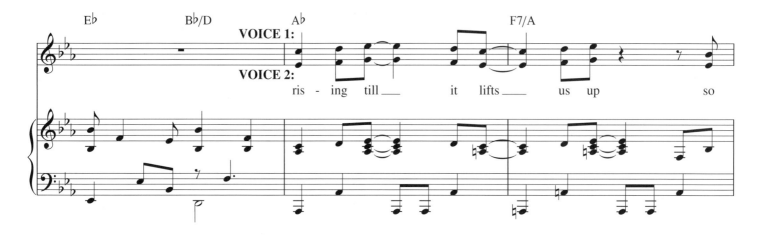

ris - ing till __ it lifts __ us up so

VOICE 1: We're break- in' free. _____

VOICE 1: We're soar - in', __ fly-
ev - 'ry-one __ can see? _____
VOICE 2: Run - nin', __ climb-

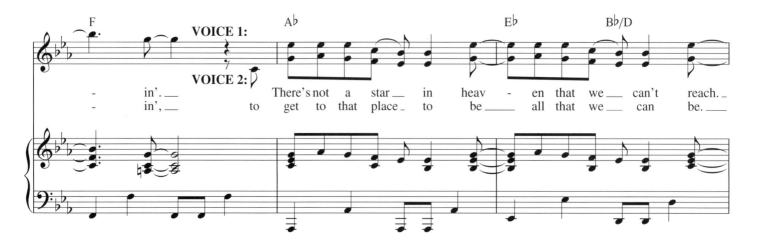

- in'. __ There's not a star __ in heav - en that we __ can't reach.
- in', __ to get to that place to be __ all that we __ can be. __

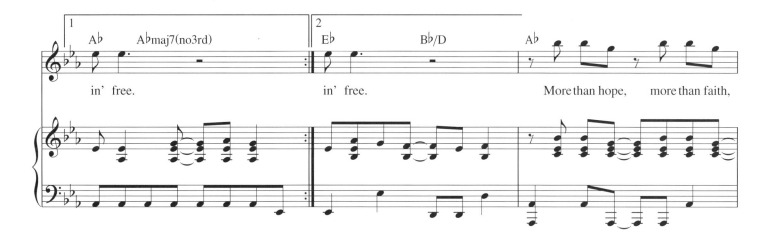

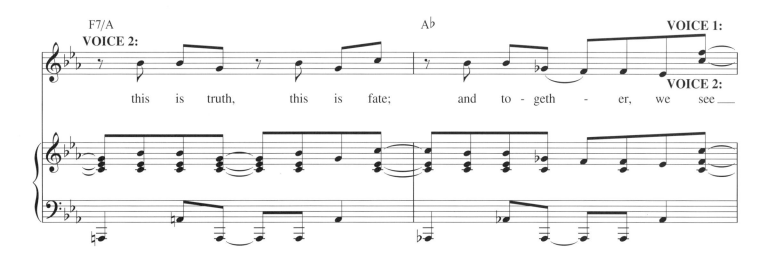

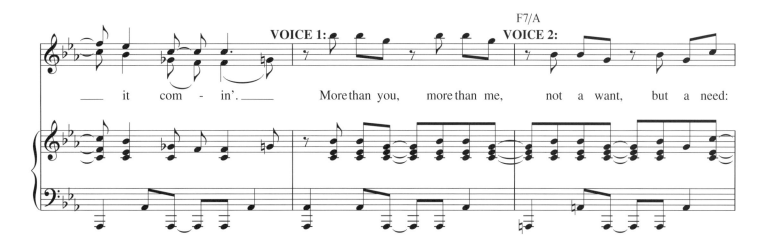

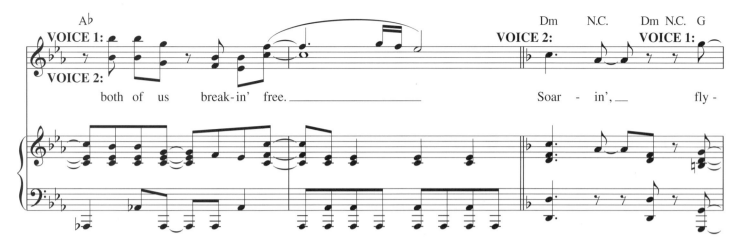

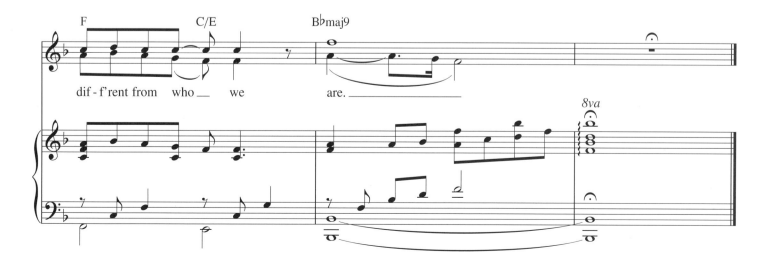

CAN YOU FEEL THE LOVE TONIGHT

Disney Presents *The Lion King: The Broadway Musical*

Music by ELTON JOHN
Lyrics by TIM RICE

*A duet for Simba and Nala in the show.

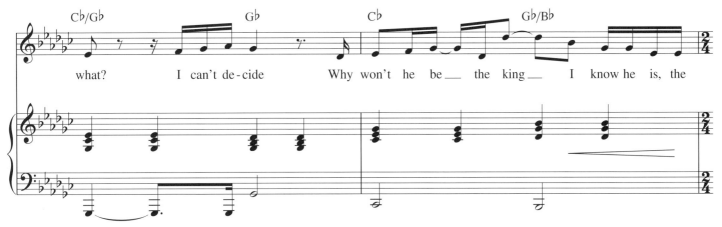

what?   I can't de-cide   Why won't he be ___ the king ___ I know he is, the

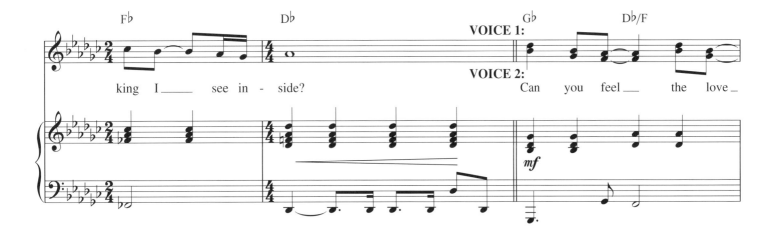

king I ___ see in - side?   Can you feel ___ the love ___

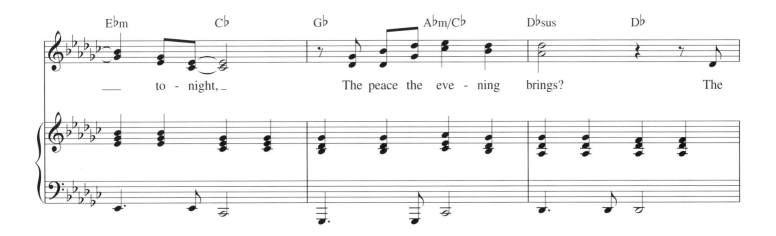

___ to - night, _   The peace the eve - ning brings?   The

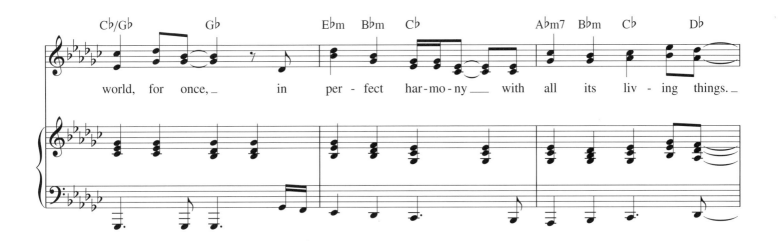

world, for once, _   in per - fect har-mo-ny ___ with all its liv - ing things. _

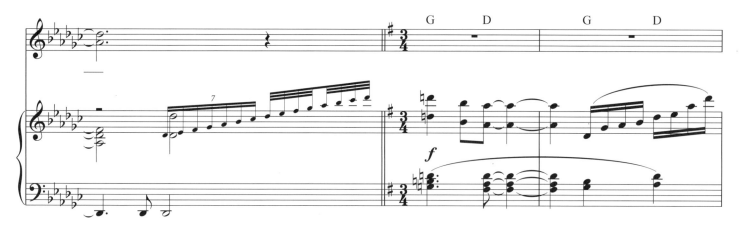

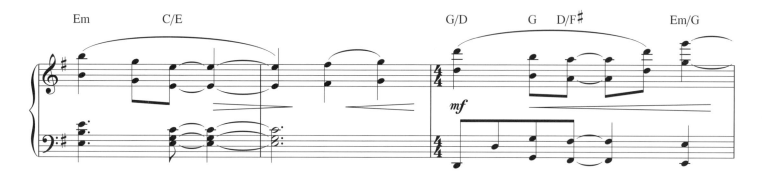

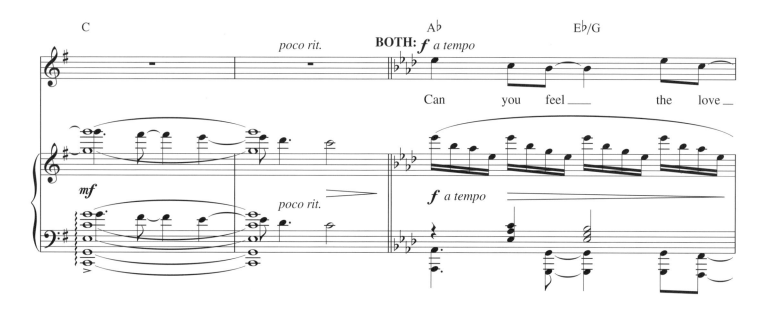

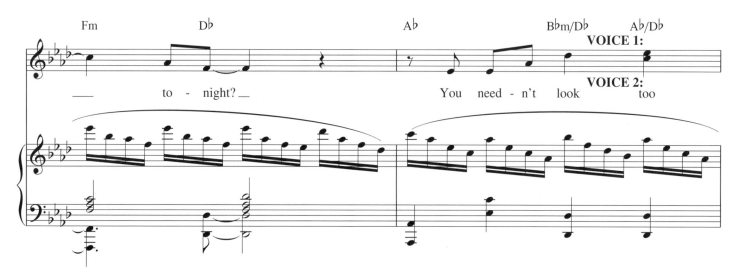

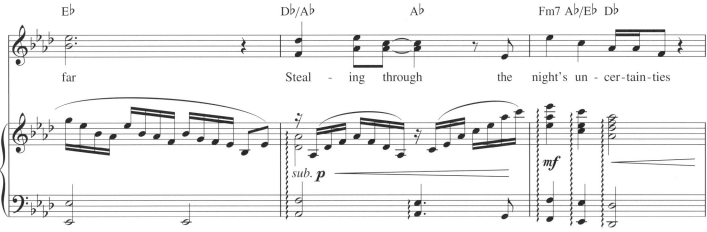

far
Steal - ing through the night's un-cer-tain-ties

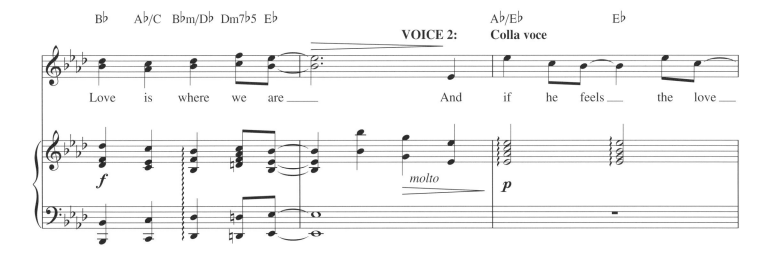

Love is where we are ___ And if he feels ___ the love ___

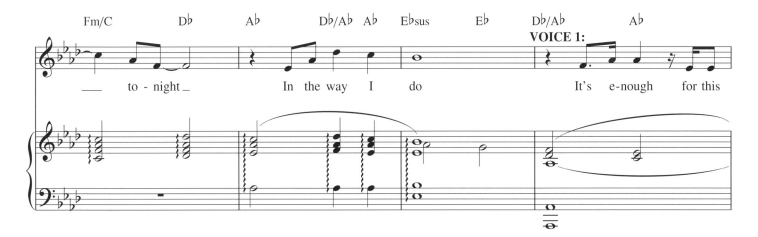

___ to - night ___ In the way I do It's e-nough for this

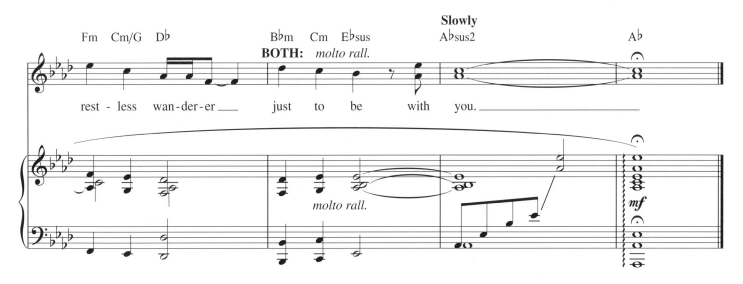

rest - less wan-der-er ___ just to be with you. _____

CHIM CHIM CHER-EE
(Rooftop Duet)
from Walt Disney's *Mary Poppins: The Broadway Musical*

Words and Music by RICHARD M. SHERMAN
and ROBERT B. SHERMAN

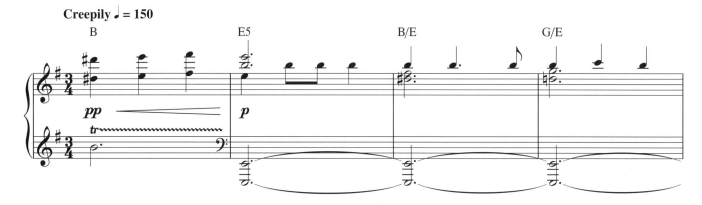

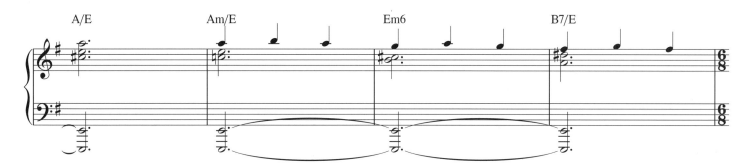

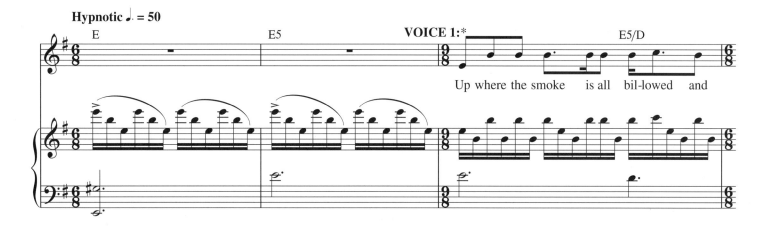

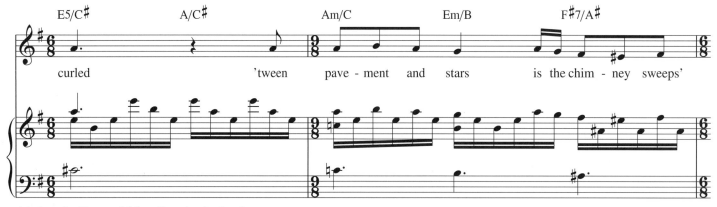

*A duet for Bert and Mary Poppins in the show.

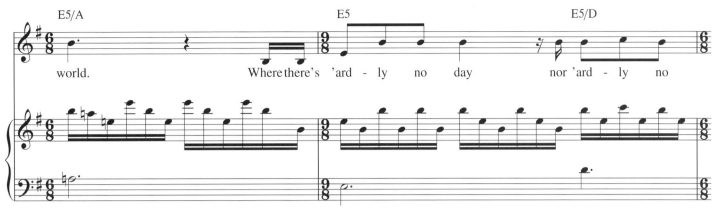

world. Where there's 'ard - ly no day nor 'ard - ly no

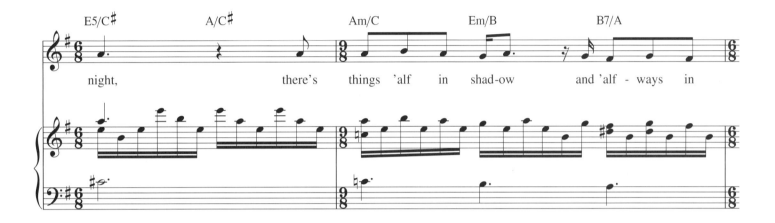

night, there's things 'alf in shad-ow and 'alf - ways in

light. On the roof - tops of Lon - don...

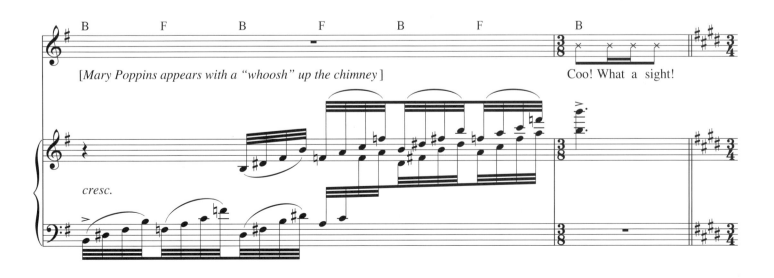

[*Mary Poppins appears with a "whoosh" up the chimney*]

Coo! What a sight!

cresc.

With motion ♩ = 180

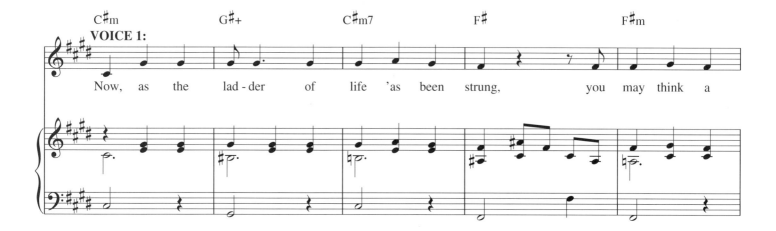

Oh. So you're a sweep now, are you?

Now, as the lad-der of life 'as been strung, you may think a

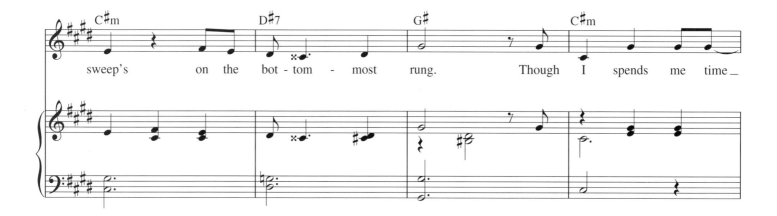

sweep's on the bot-tom - most rung. Though I spends me time —

— in the ash - es and smoke, in this 'ole wide

world there's no 'ap-pi - er bloke.

VOICE 1:

VOICE 2:

Chim chim-i-ney, chim chim-i-ney, chim chim che -

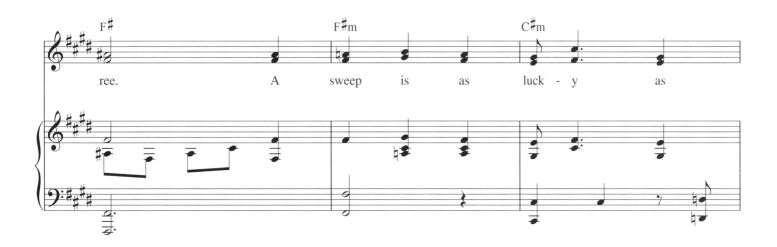

ree. A sweep is as luck-y as

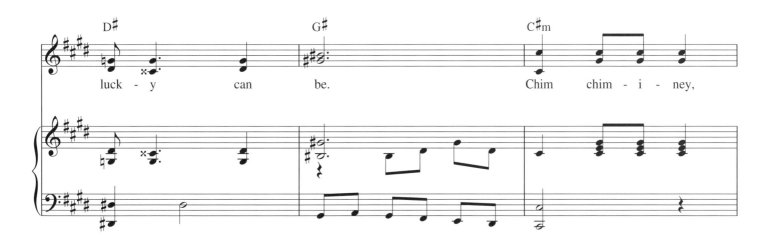

luck-y can be. Chim chim-i-ney,

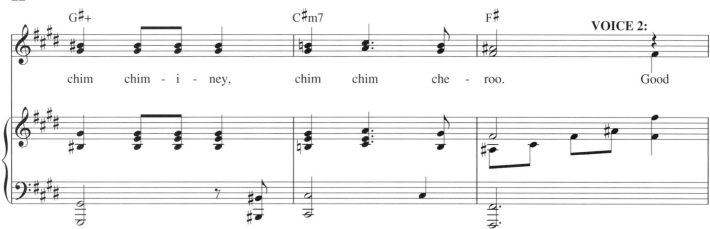

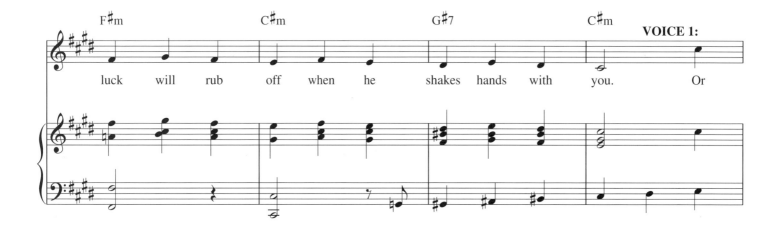

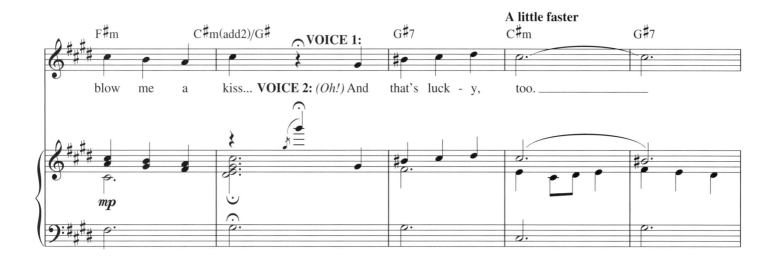

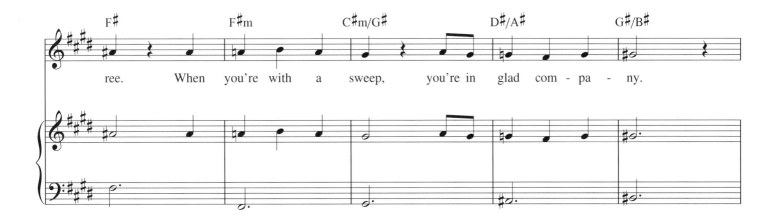

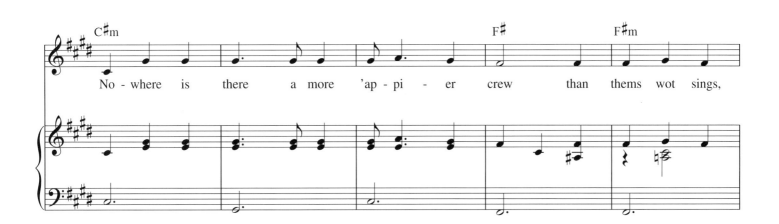

"Chim chim che-ree, chim che-roo." Chim chim-i-ney,

chim chim, che-ree, chim... Cheer-i-o. *Keep an eye on them for me.*

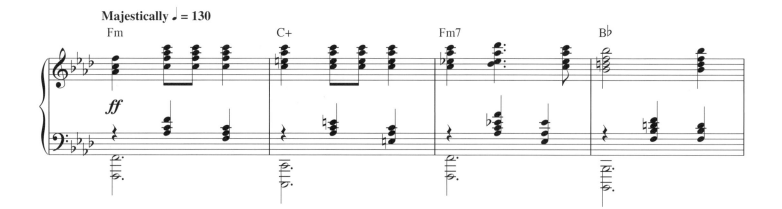

Majestically ♩ = 130

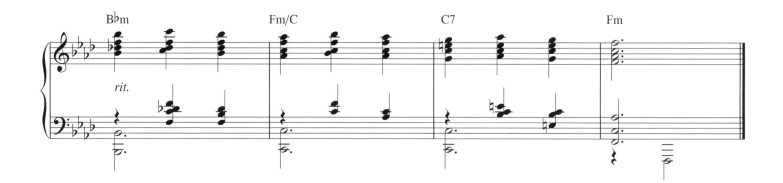

I SEE THE LIGHT
from Walt Disney Pictures' *Tangled*

Music by ALAN MENKEN
Lyrics by GLENN SLATER

All those days, watch-ing from the win-dows.
Now I'm here, blink-ing in the star-light.

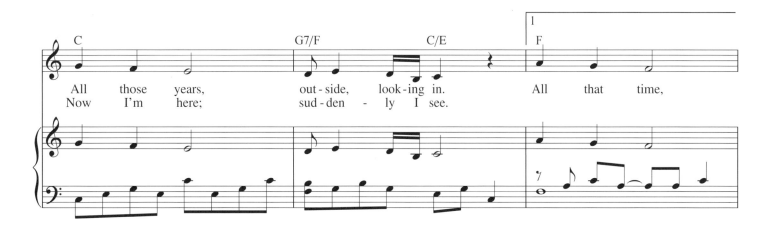

All those years, out-side, look-ing in.
Now I'm here; sud-den-ly I see.

All that time,

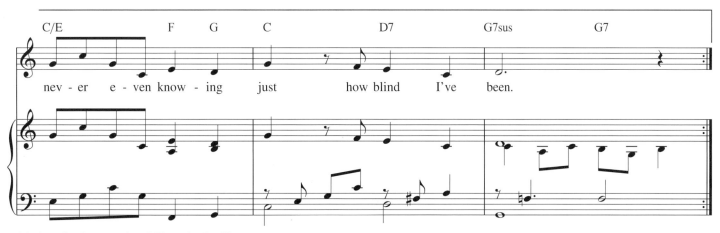

nev-er e-ven know-ing just how blind I've been.

*A duet for Rapunzel and Flynn in the film.

Standing here, it's, oh, so clear I'm where I'm meant to

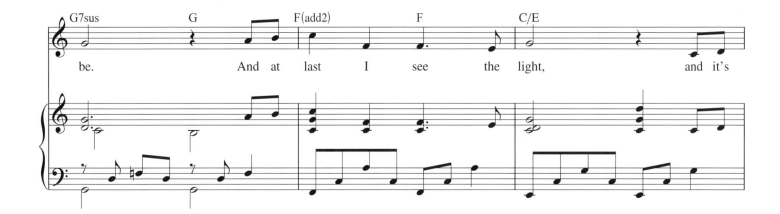

be. And at last I see the light, and it's

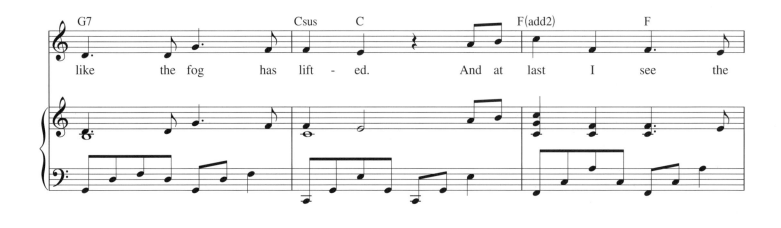

like the fog has lift - ed. And at last I see the

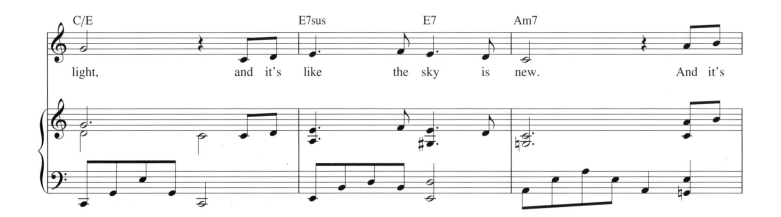

light, and it's like the sky is new. And it's

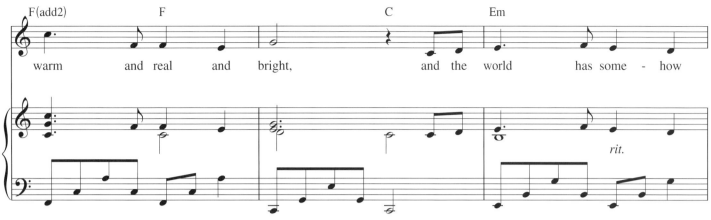

warm and real and bright, and the world has some - how

shift - ed. All at once,

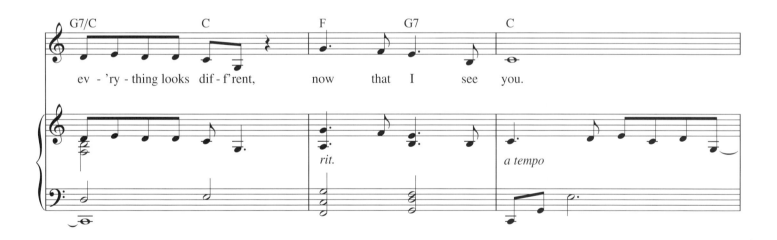

ev - 'ry-thing looks dif - f'rent, now that I see you.

All those days, chas-ing down a day-dream. All those years

living in a blur. All that time, nev-er tru-ly see-ing

things the way they were. Now she's here,

shin-ing in the star-light. Now she's here; sud-den-ly I know:

if she's here, it's___ crys-tal clear I'm where I'm meant to

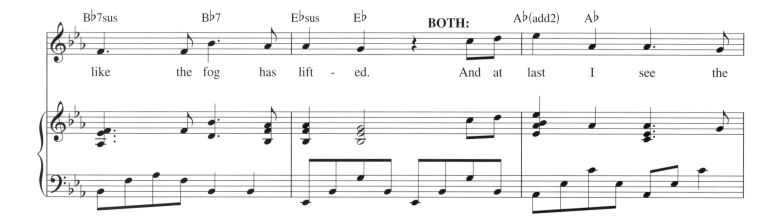

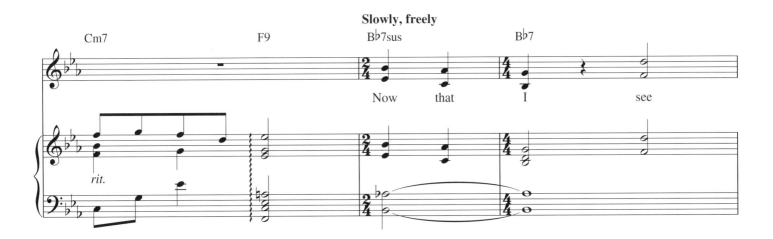

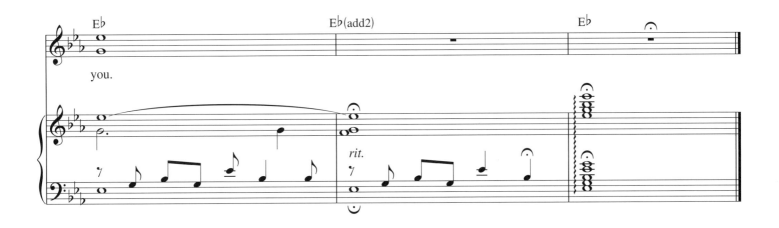

CHOW DOWN
Disney Presents *The Lion King: The Broadway Musical*

Music by ELTON JOHN
Lyrics by TIM RICE

*A duet for Banzai and Shenzi in the show.

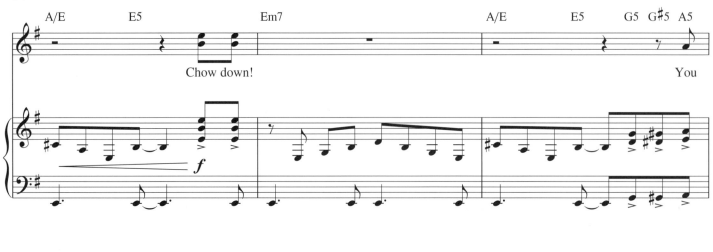

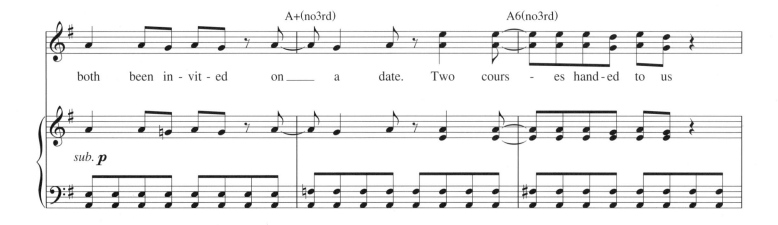

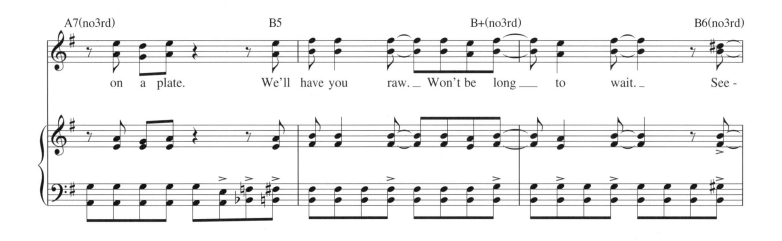

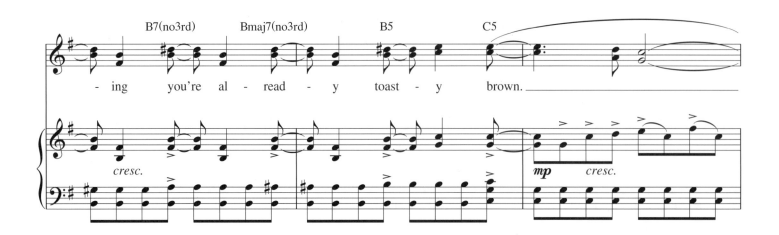

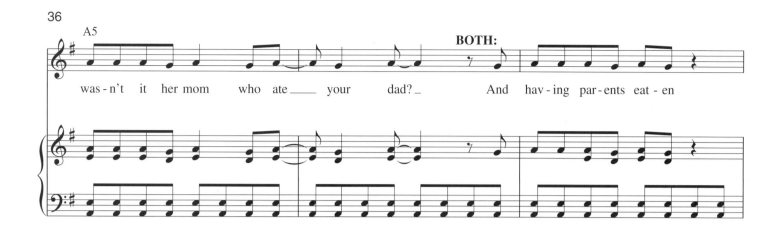

was-n't it her mom who ate ___ your dad? ___ And hav-ing par-ents eat-en

makes us mad. ___ We're gon-na set-tle up the score ___ a tad. We've nev-

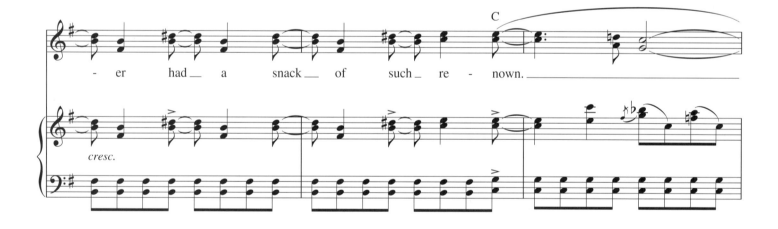

-er had ___ a snack ___ of such ___ re-nown. ___

Chow down! Ch - ch - ch - ch - ch Chow down!

FEED THE BIRDS
from Walt Disney's *Mary Poppins: The Broadway Musical*

Music and Lyrics by RICHARD M. SHERMAN
and ROBERT B. SHERMAN

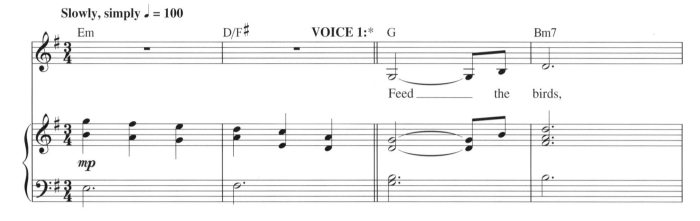

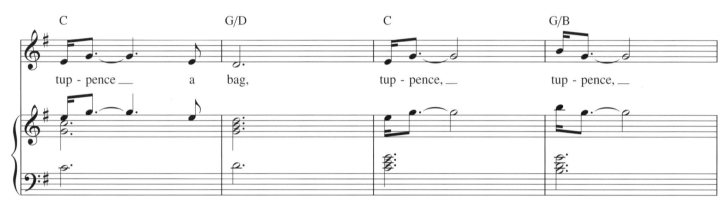

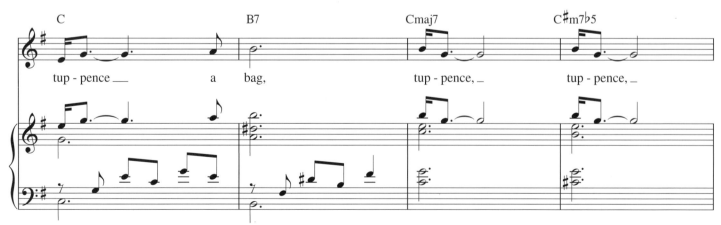

*A duet for the Bird Woman and Mary Poppins in the show.

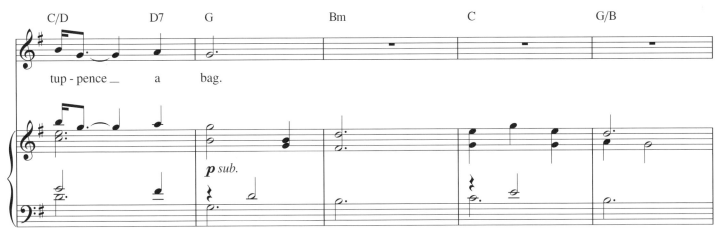

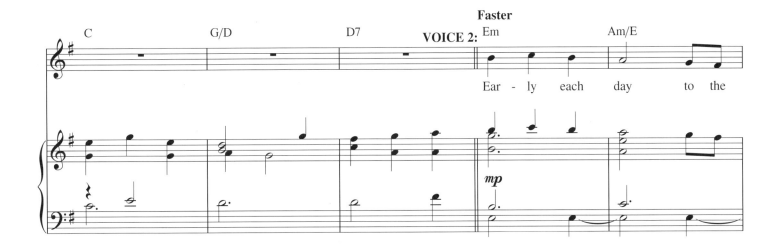

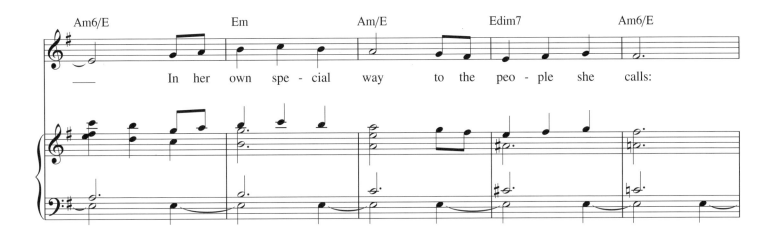

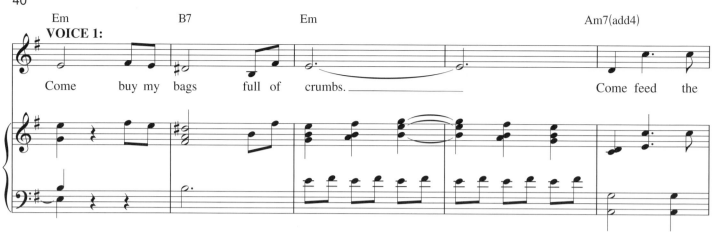

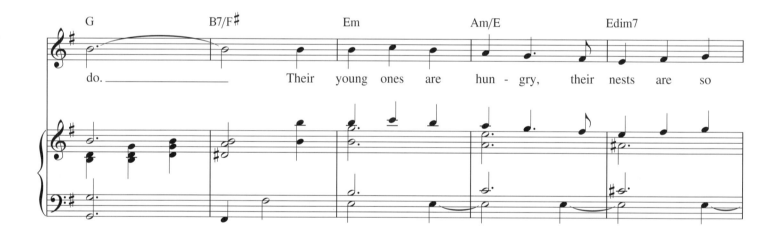

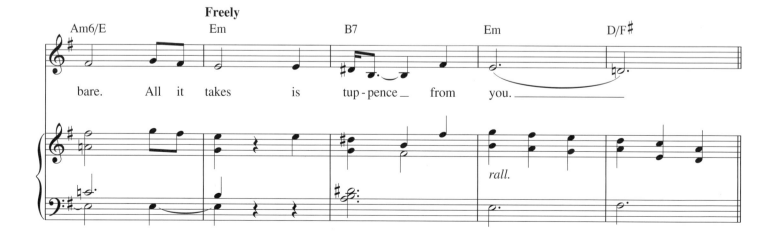

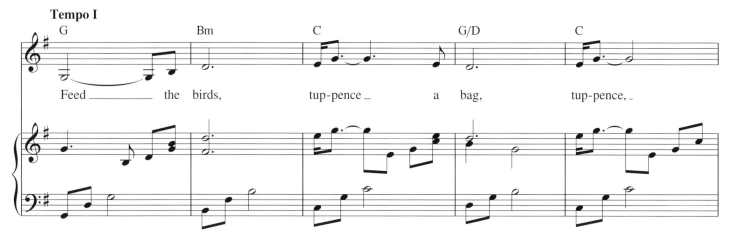

Tempo I

Feed _____ the birds, tup-pence _ a bag, tup-pence, _

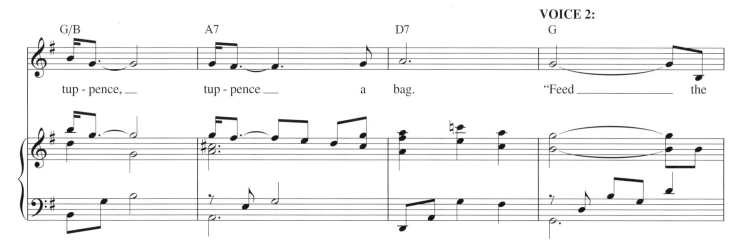

VOICE 2:

tup - pence, _ tup - pence _ a bag. "Feed _____ the

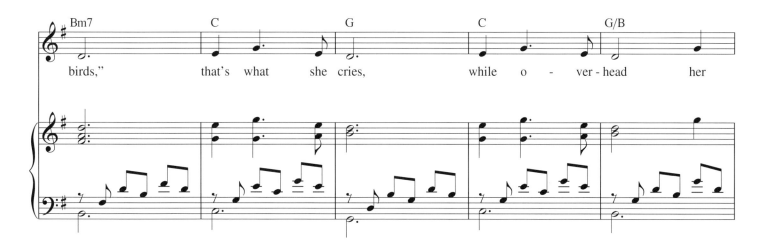

birds," that's what she cries, while o - ver - head her

Slightly faster

birds fill the skies. All a - round the ca - the - dral, the saints and a -

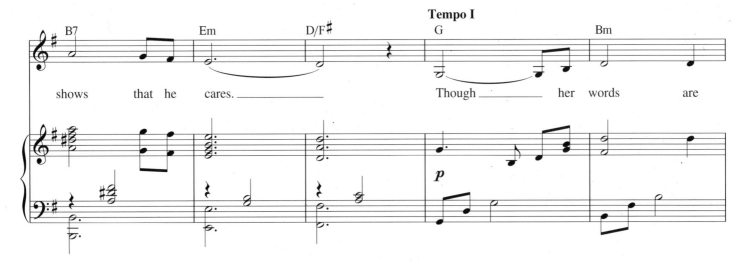

D7
VOICE 1:
G
Bm7
C
you. Feed the birds, tup - pence a
mp
B7
Cmaj7
BOTH:
C♯m7♭5
C/D
D7
bag. Tup-pence, tup-pence, tup-pence a
Em
A7
Slower, freely
Cmaj7
VOICE 1:
bag.
Tup-pence,
C♯m7♭5
C/D
D7
G
tup - pence, tup - pence a bag.
rit.

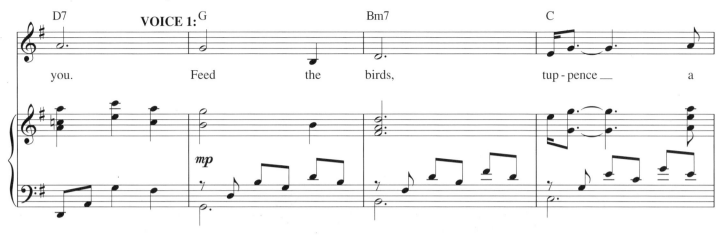

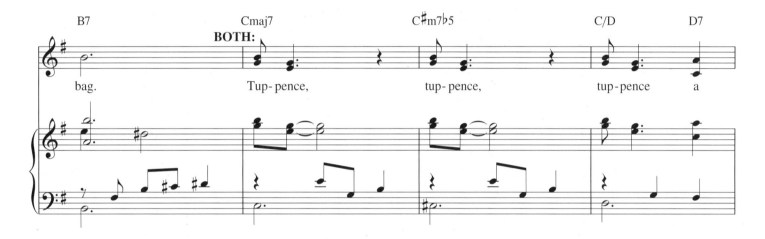

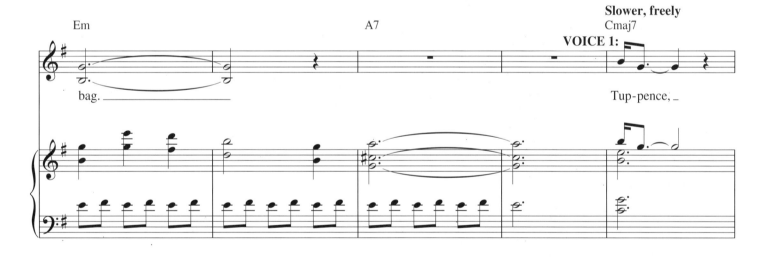

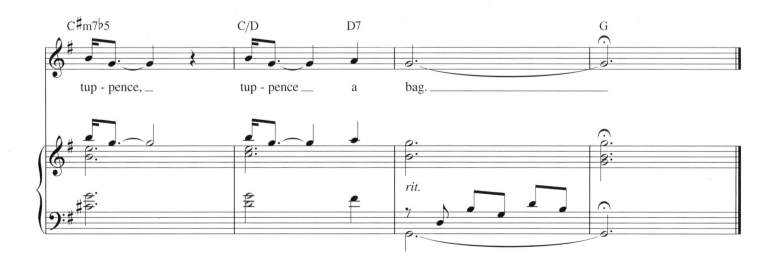

IF I NEVER KNEW YOU
(Love Theme from Pocahontas)
from Walt Disney's *Pocahontas*

Music by ALAN MENKEN
Lyrics by STEPHEN SCHWARTZ

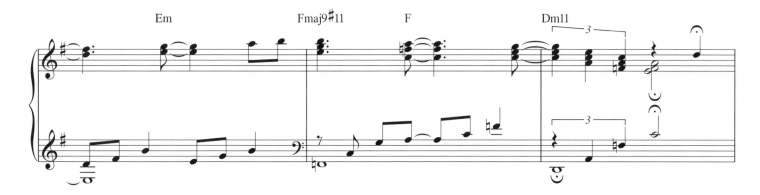

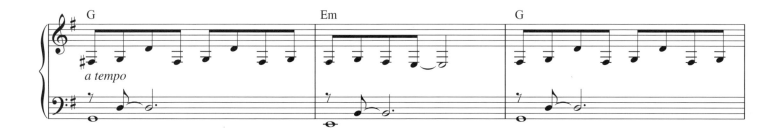

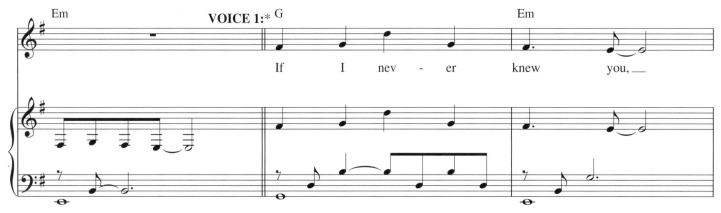

If I nev - er knew you, __

*A duet for John Smith and Pocahontas in the film.

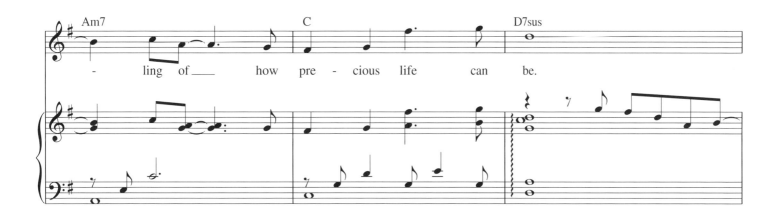

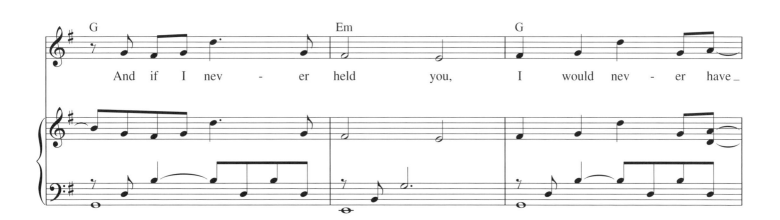

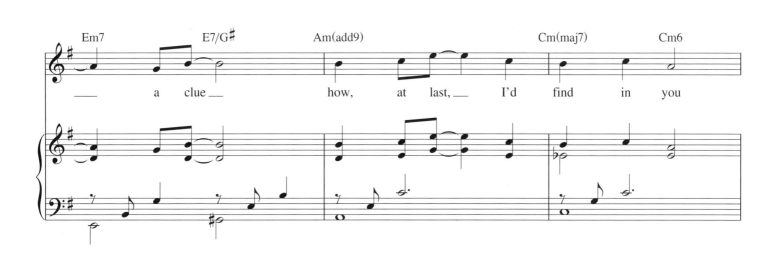

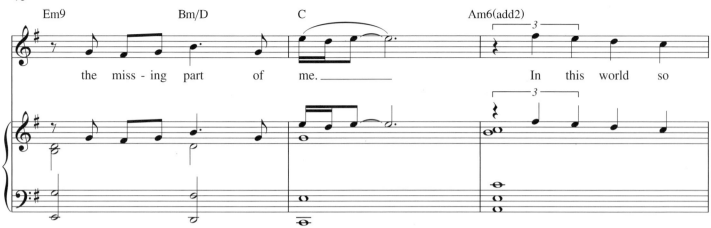

the miss-ing part of me. In this world so

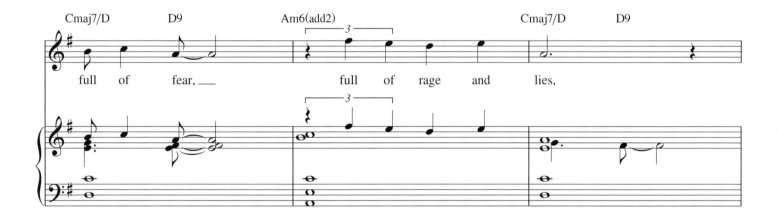

full of fear, full of rage and lies,

I can see the truth so clear in your eyes, so

dry your eyes. And I'm so grate-ful to you.

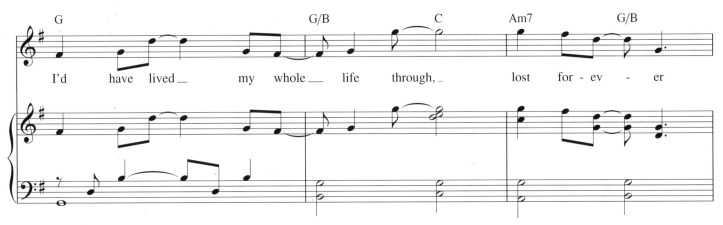

I'd have lived ___ my whole ___ life through, ___ lost for - ev - er

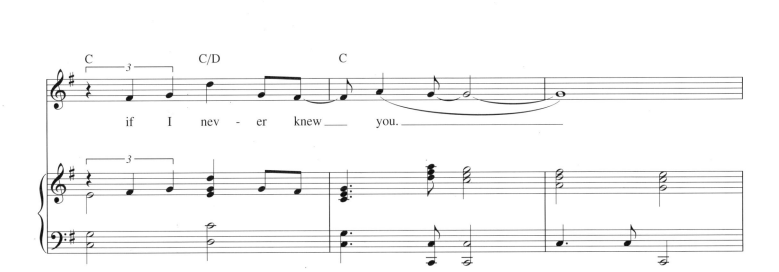

if I nev - er knew ___ you. ___

VOICE 2:

If I nev - er knew you,

I'd be safe ___ but half ___ as real, nev - er know - ing I ___

could feel ___ a love so strong ___ and true.

I'm so grate - ful to you. I'd have lived ___ my whole ___

___ life through, lost for - ev - er if I nev - er knew

VOICE 1: I thought our love would be so beau - ti - ful.

you. ___

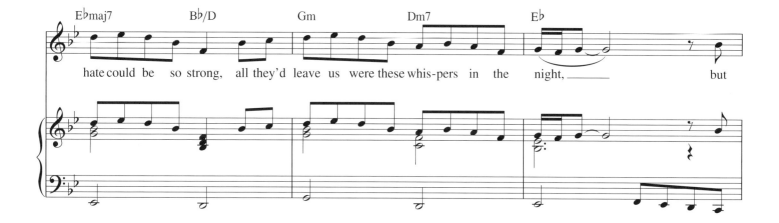

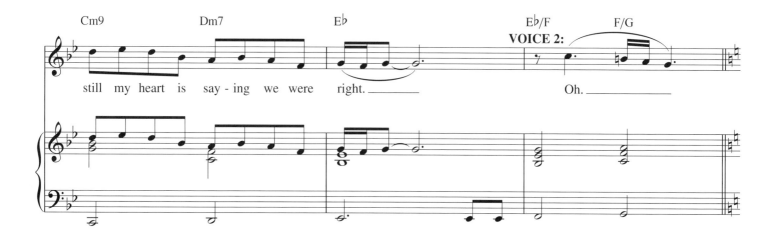

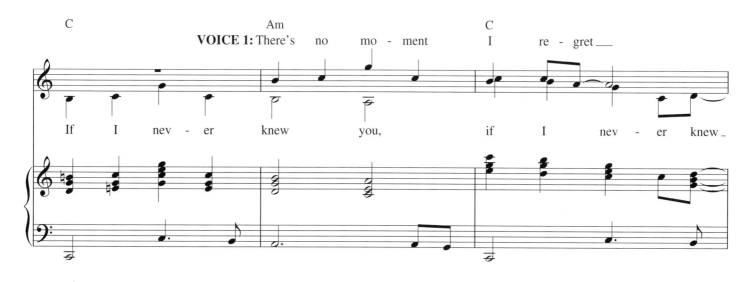

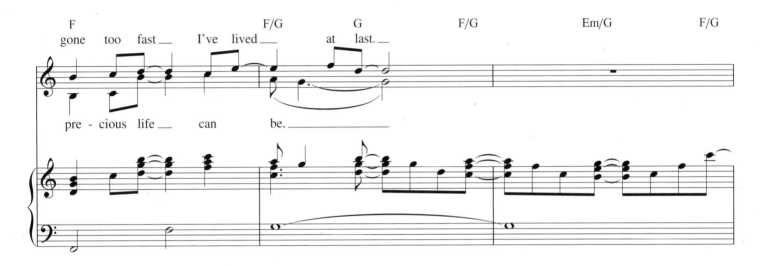

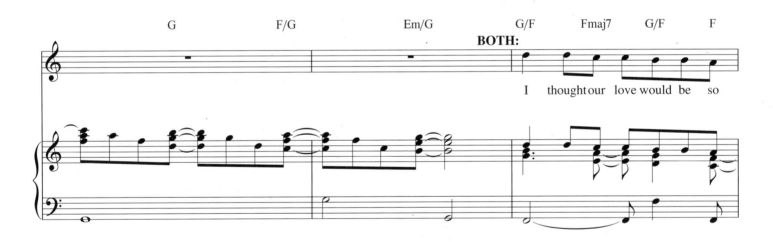

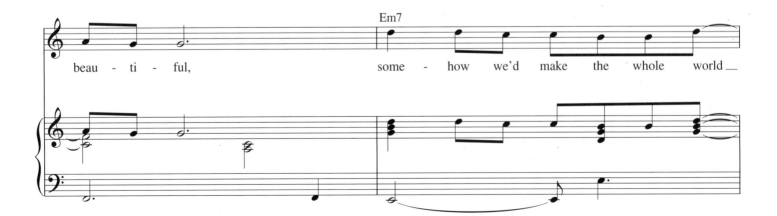

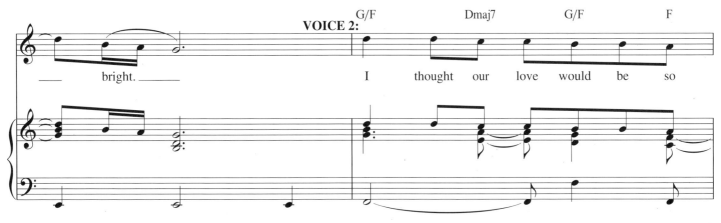

I thought our love would be so

beau-ti-ful, we'd turn the dark-ness in-to light. And

still my heart is say-ing we were right. We were right. And

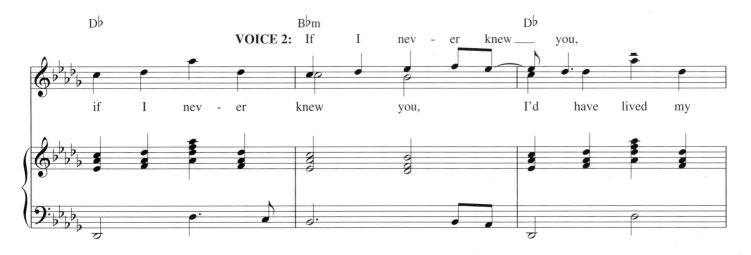

If I nev-er knew you, if I nev-er knew you, I'd have lived my

VOICE 2:

whole life through empty as ___ the sky, ___

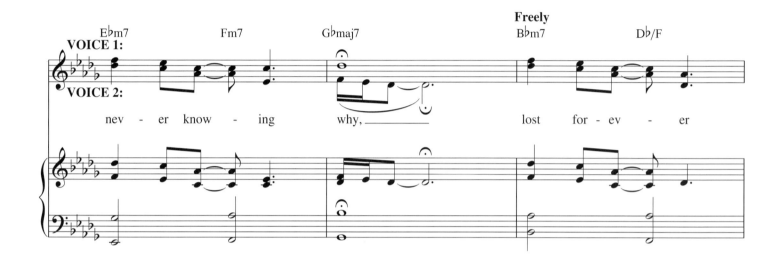

VOICE 1:
VOICE 2:

nev - er know - ing why, ___ lost for - ev - er

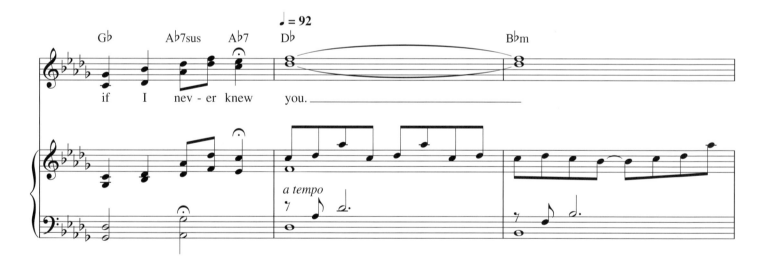

if I nev - er knew you. ___

a tempo

rit.

LOVE WILL FIND A WAY
from Walt Disney's *The Lion King II: Simba's Pride*

Lyrics by JACK FELDMAN
Music by TOM SNOW

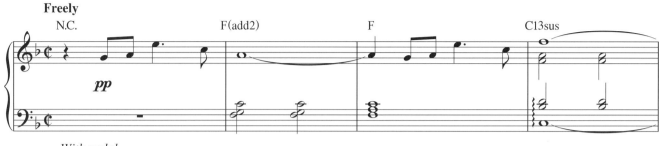

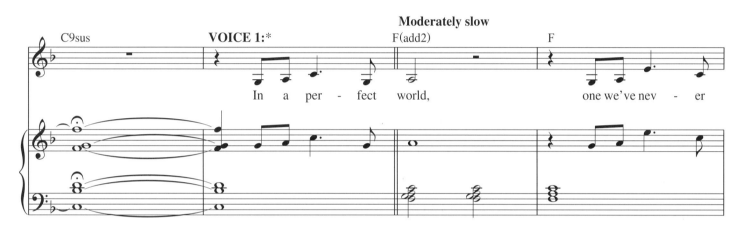

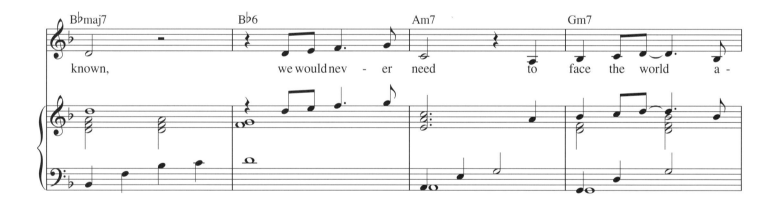

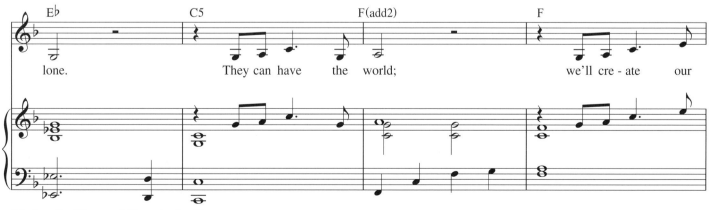

*A duet for Kiara and Kovu in the film.

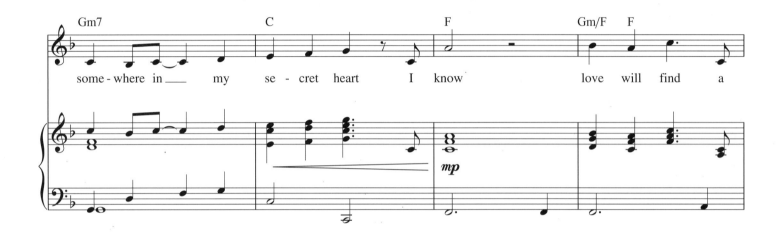

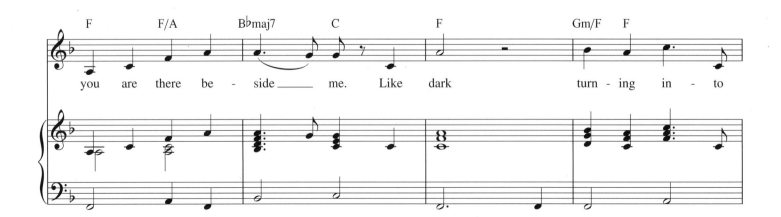

day, some-how we'll come through. Now that I've found

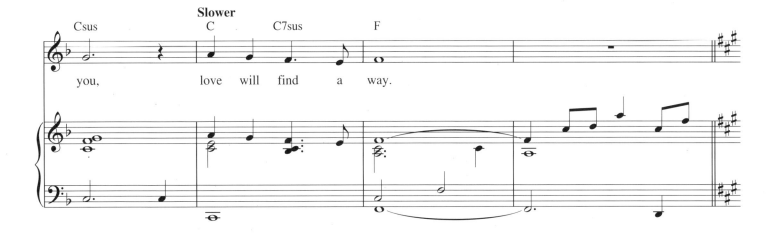

Slower

you, love will find a way.

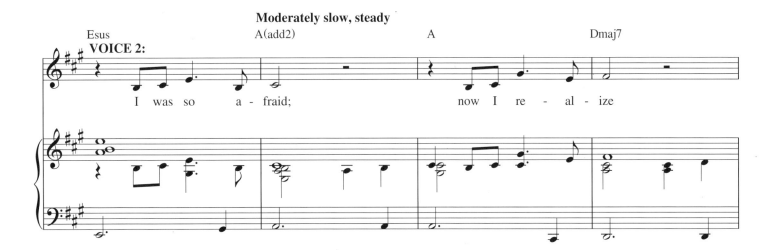

Moderately slow, steady

VOICE 2: I was so a-fraid; now I re-al-ize

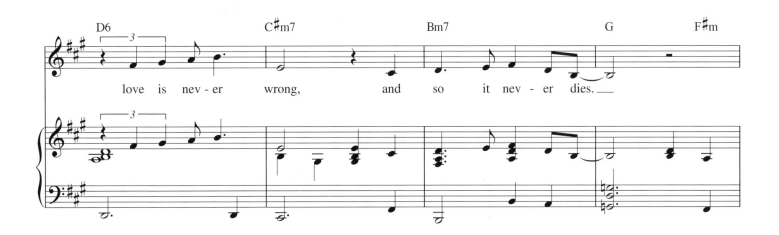

love is nev-er wrong, and so it nev-er dies.

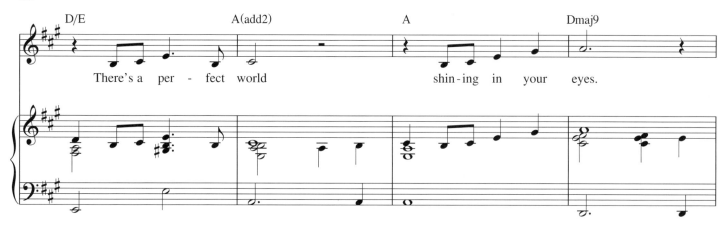

There's a per - fect world shin-ing in your eyes.

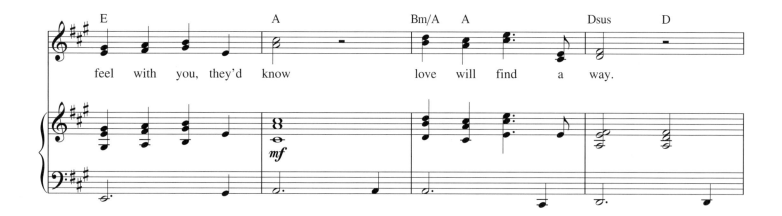

And if on - ly they could feel it too, the hap - pi - ness _ I

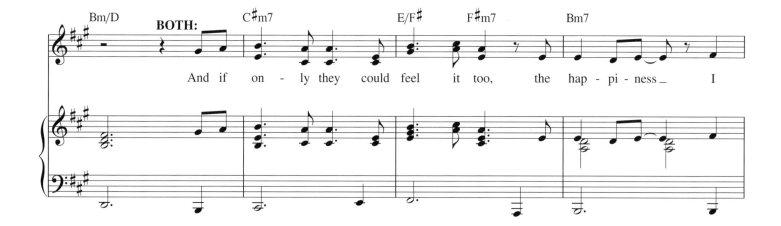

feel with you, they'd know love will find a way.

An - y - where _ we go we're _ home if we are there to -

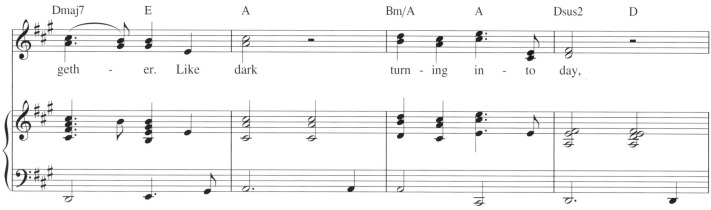

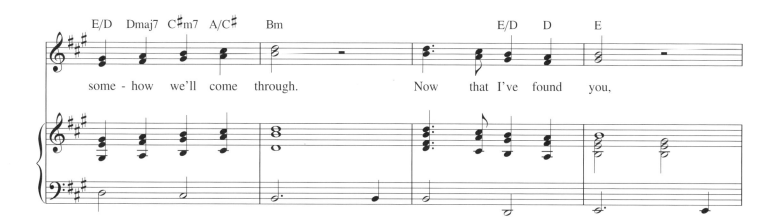

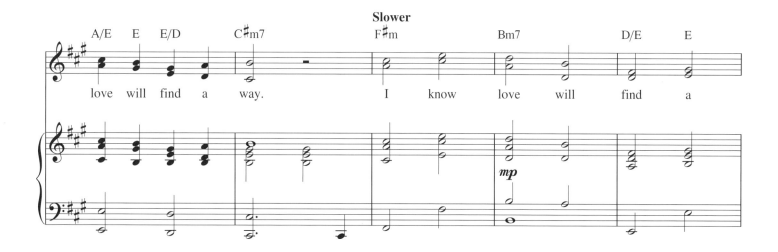

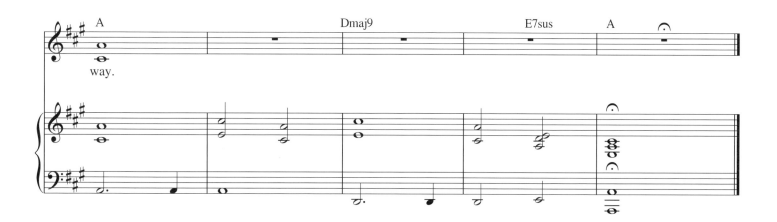

LOVE IS AN OPEN DOOR
from Disney's Animated Feature *Frozen*

Music and Lyrics by KRISTEN ANDERSON-LOPEZ
and ROBERT LOPEZ

Moderately, with a cheesy groove

*A duet for Anna and Hans in the film.

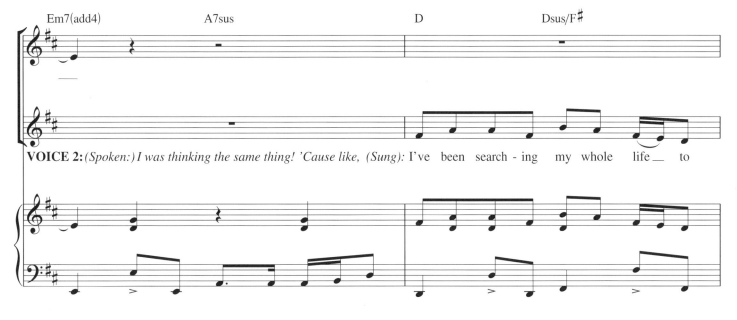

VOICE 2: *(Spoken:) I was thinking the same thing! 'Cause like, (Sung):* I've been search - ing my whole life __ to

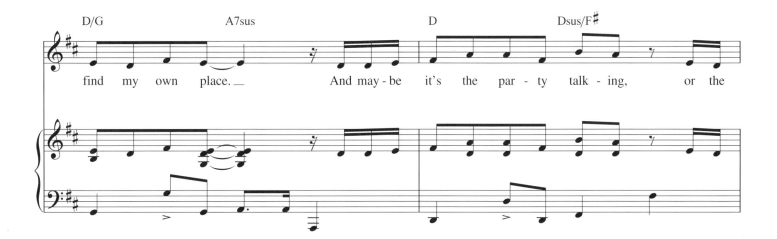

find my own place. __ And may - be it's the par - ty talk - ing, or the

VOICE 1:

But with you, _____

VOICE 2:

cho - c'late fon - due... _____ but with you, __ I found my _____

I see your face, and it's noth-ing like ___ I've ev-er known ___ be -

___ place. and it's noth-ing like ___ I've ev-er known ___ be -

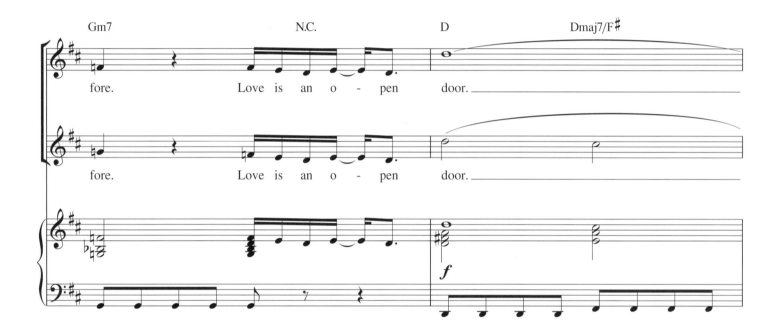

fore. Love is an o - pen door. ___

fore. Love is an o - pen door. ___

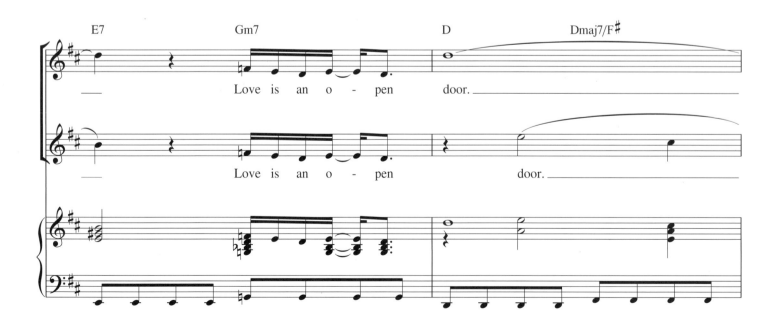

Love is an o - pen door. ___

Love is an o - pen door. ___

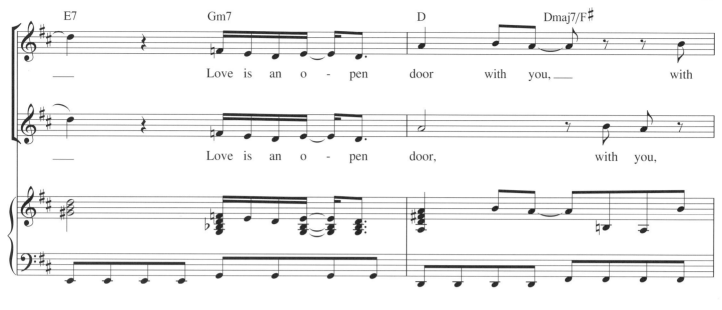

Love is an o - pen door with you, ___ with

Love is an o - pen door, with you,

you! Love is an o - pen door. ___

with you!! Love is an o - pen door. ___

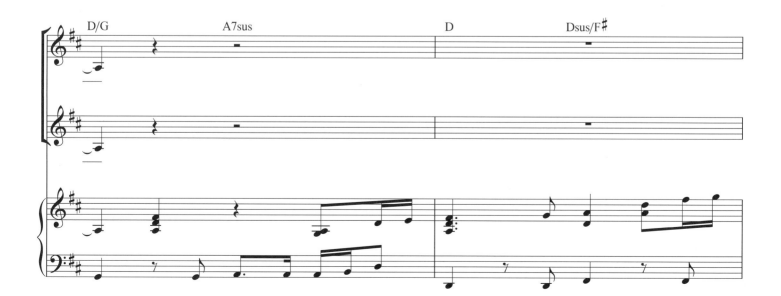

62

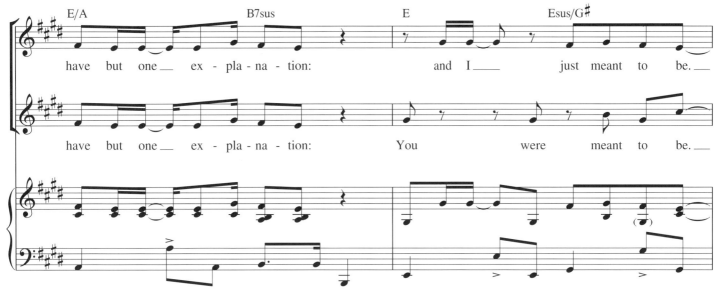

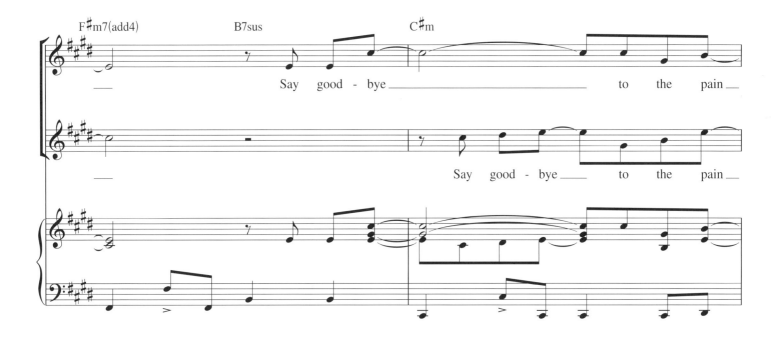

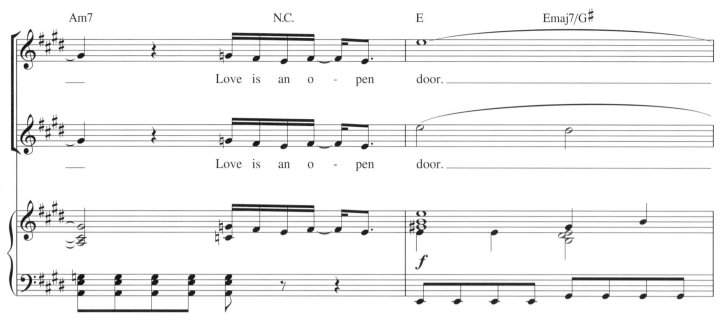

NO MATTER WHAT
from Walt Disney's *Beauty and the Beast: The Broadway Musical*

Music by ALAN MENKEN
Lyrics by TIM RICE

*A duet for Maurice and Belle in the show.

In all you say or do, you could-n't make it plain- er. You are your moth-er's daugh-ter.

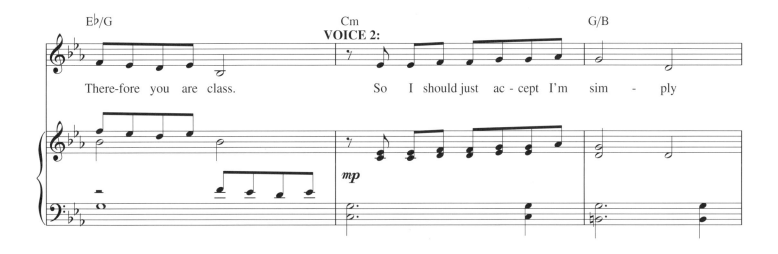

There-fore you are class. So I should just ac-cept I'm sim - ply

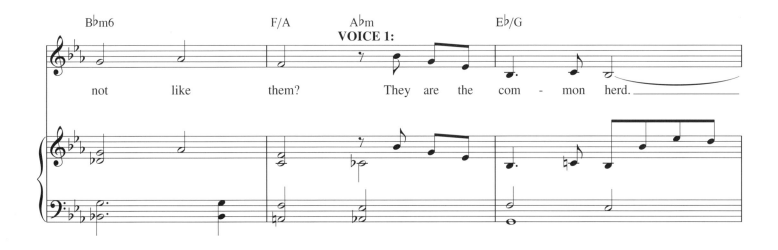

not like them? They are the com - mon herd. _____

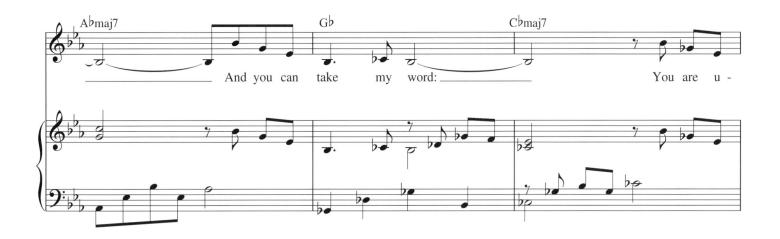

_____ And you can take my word: _____ You are u -

Faster in 2

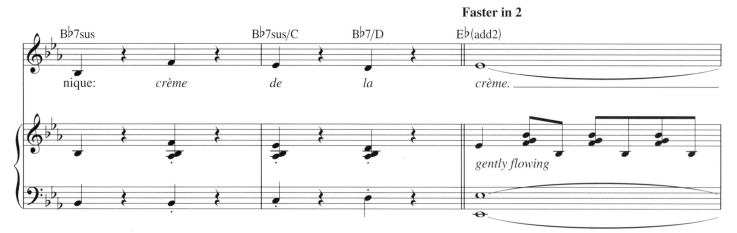

nique: _crème_ _de_ _la_ _crème._

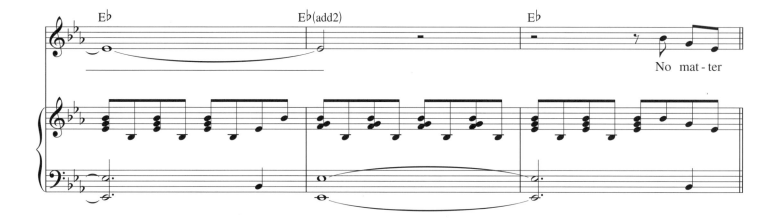

No mat - ter

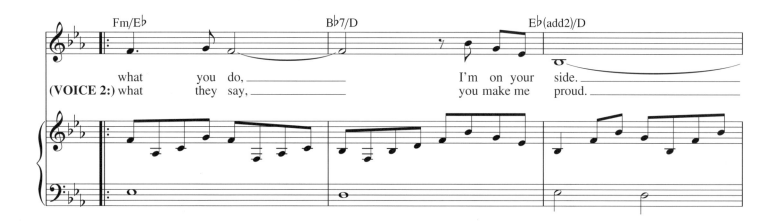

(VOICE 2:) what you do, _____ I'm on your side. _____
what they say, _____ you make me proud. _____

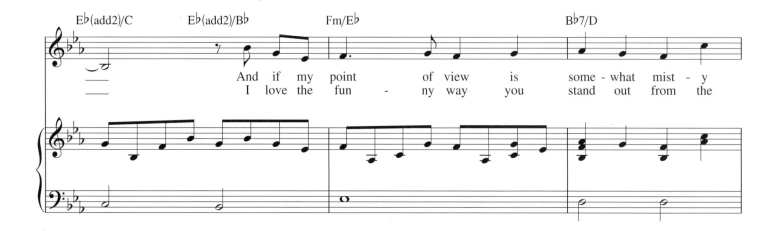

And if my point of view is some - what mist - y
I love the fun - ny way you stand out from the

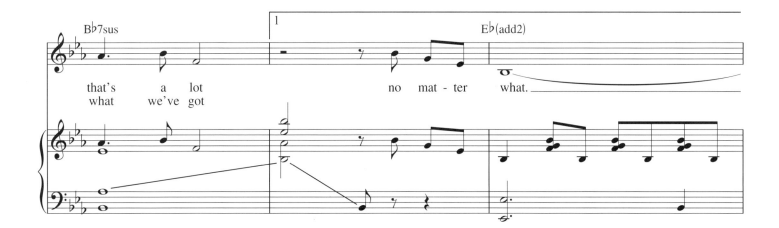

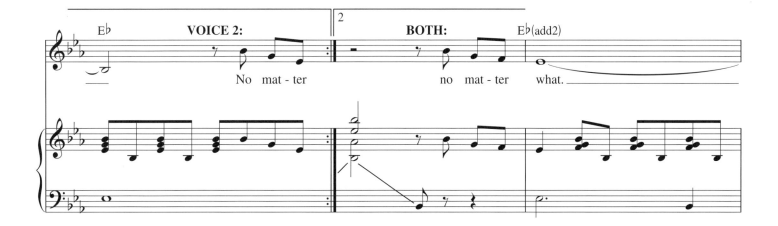

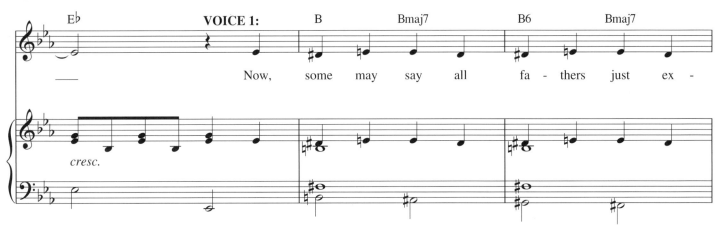

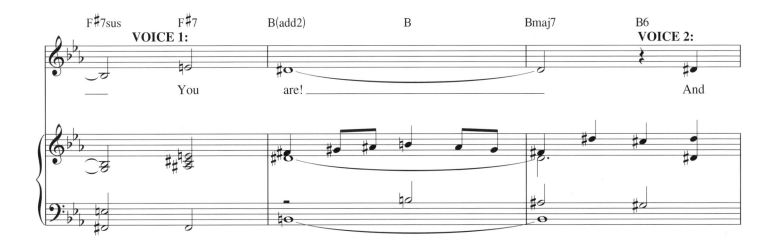

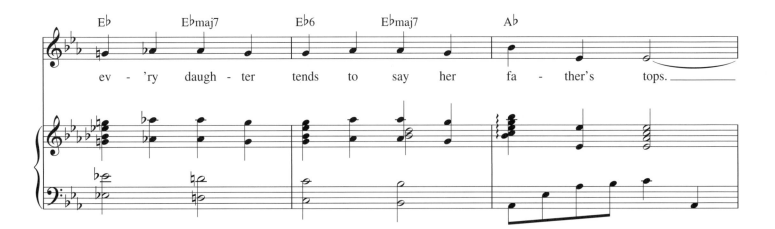

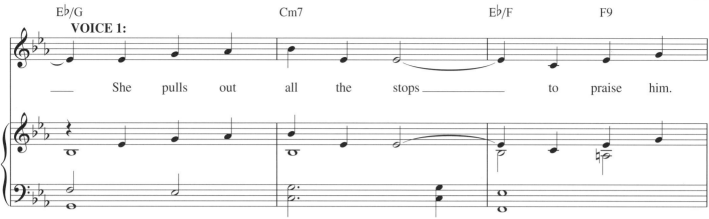

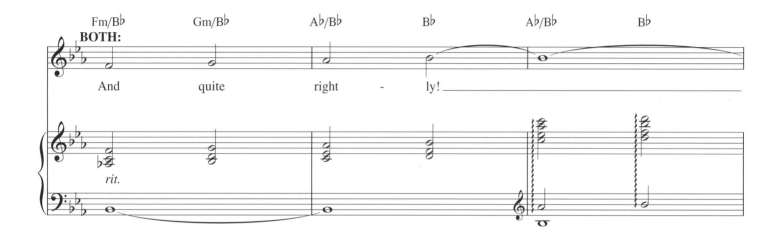

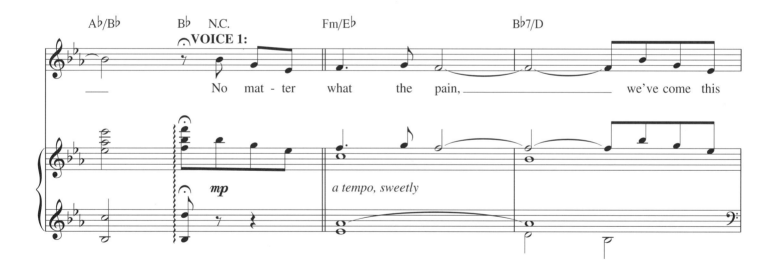

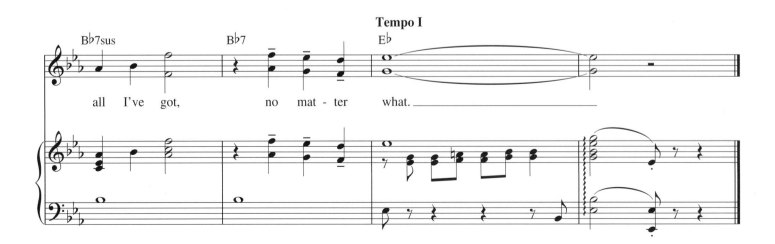

SOMETHING THERE
from Walt Disney's *Beauty and the Beast: The Broadway Musical*

Lyrics by HOWARD ASHMAN
Music by ALAN MENKEN

*A duet for Belle and the Beast in the show.

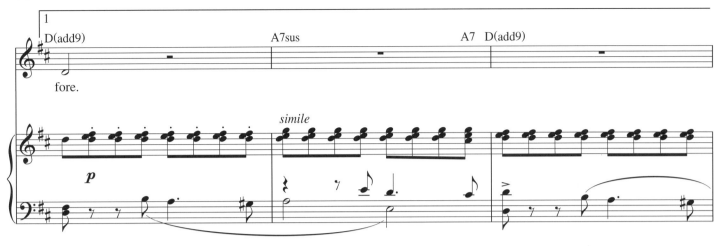

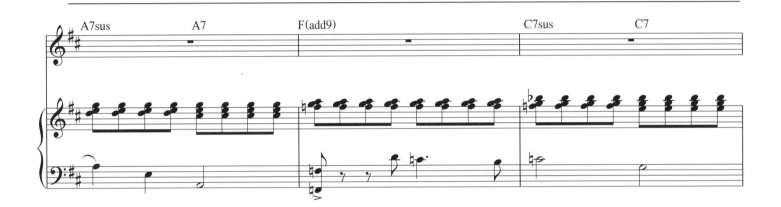

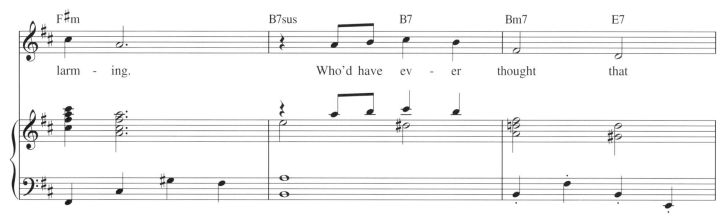

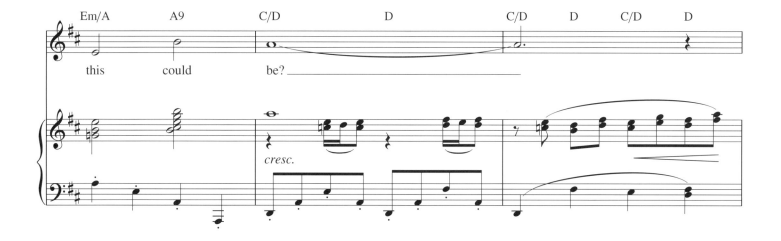

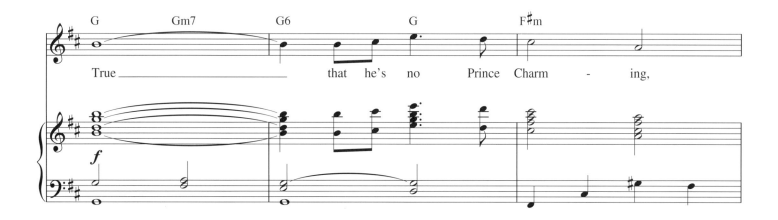

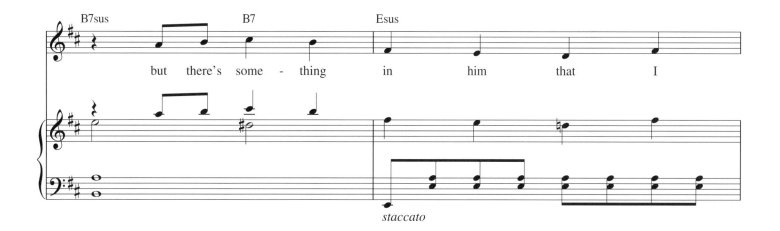

76

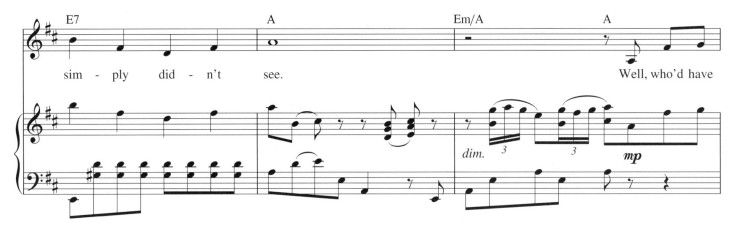

sim - ply did - n't see.   Well, who'd have

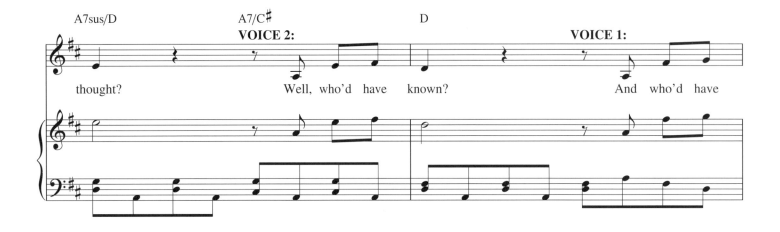

thought?   Well, who'd have known?   And who'd have

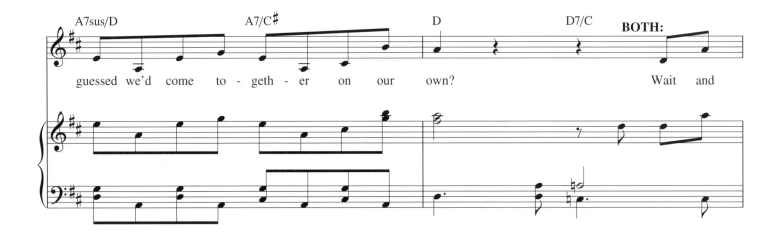

guessed we'd come to - geth - er on our own?   Wait and

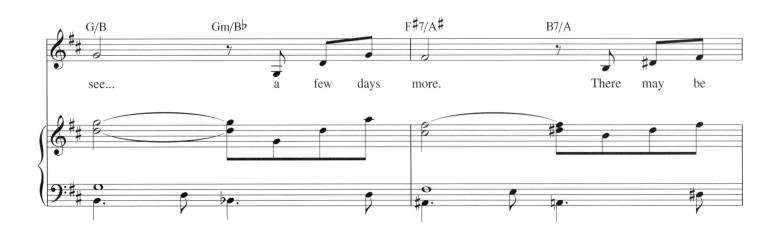

see...   a few days more.   There may be

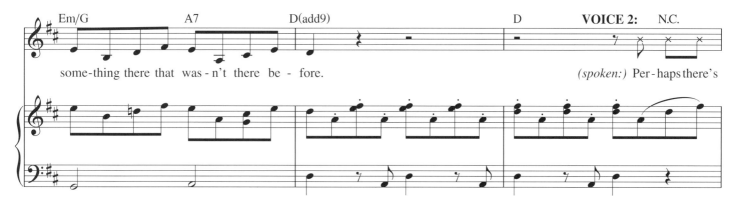

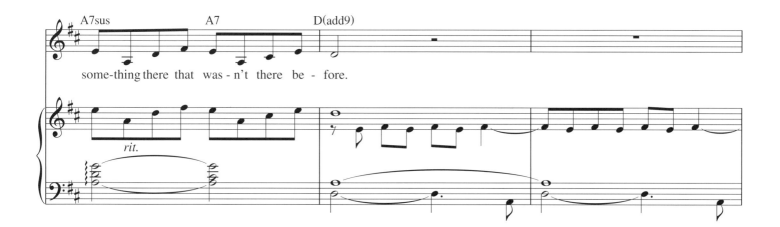

SWEET CHILD
from Walt Disney's *The Little Mermaid: A Broadway Musical*

Music by ALAN MENKEN
Lyrics by GLENN SLATER

Slitheringly slimy 2

VOICE 1:* *Poor child.*   VOICE 2: *Poor sweet child.*

VOICE 1: *She has a very serious problem, hasn't she?*   VOICE 2: *If only…*   VOICE 1: *… there were something…*

VOICE 2: *… we could do.*   VOICE 1: Sweet child, VOICE 2: poor

*A duet for Flotsam and Jetsam in the show.

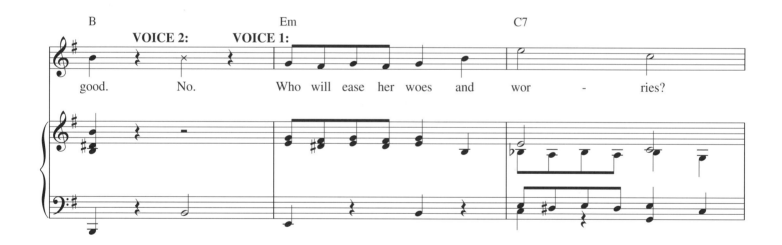

80

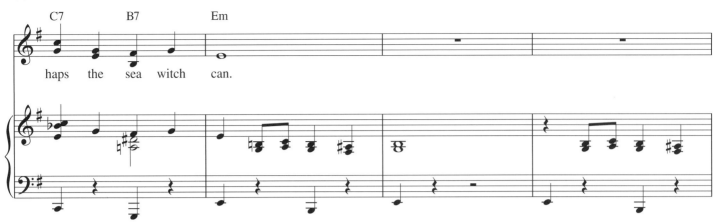

haps the sea witch can.

VOICE 1: She knows your dreams. VOICE 2: She'll grant your pray'r.

VOICE 1: She'll cast a charm, a ti-ny spell. VOICE 2: Why the a-larm? VOICE 1: No one-'ll tell, no one-'ll

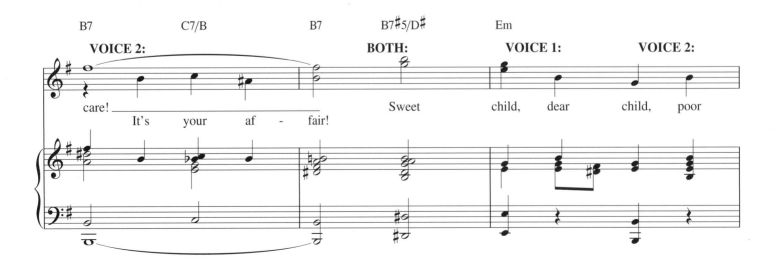

VOICE 2: care! It's your af-fair! BOTH: Sweet VOICE 1: child, dear VOICE 2: child, poor

child, sad child! We'll bring you to her lair right now.

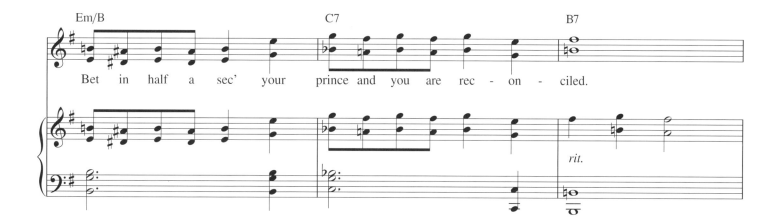

Bet in half a sec' your prince and you are rec - on - ciled.

VOICE 1: *Together...* **VOICE 2:** *... forever.* Sweet child!

WE ARE ONE
from Walt Disney's *The Lion King II: Simba's Pride*

Lyrics by MARTY PANZER and JACK FELDMAN
Music by TOM SNOW

VOICE 1:* As you go ___ through life, ___ you'll see ___ there is
VOICE 2: If there's so ___ much I ___ must be, ___ can I

so much that we ___ don't un- der- stand. ___
still just ___ be me, ___ the way I am? ___

*A duet for Simba and Kiara in the film.

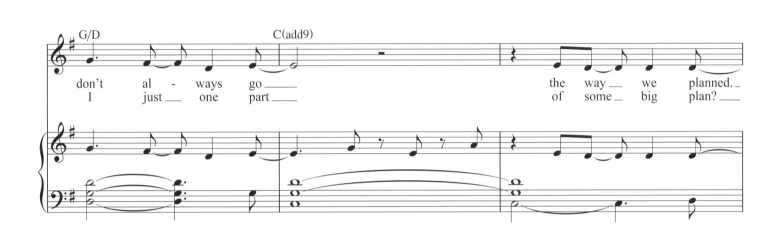

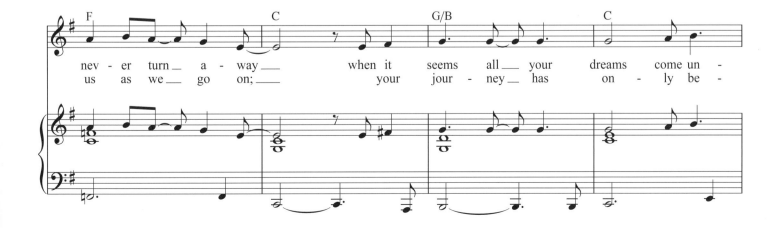

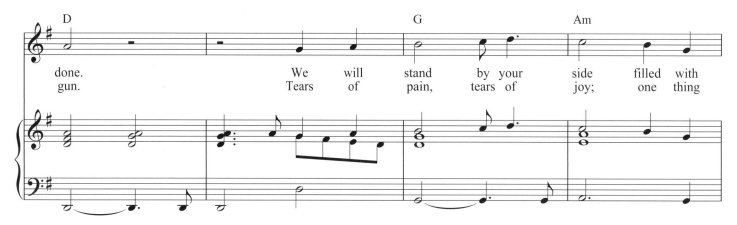

done. We will stand by your side filled with
gun. Tears of pain, tears of joy; one thing

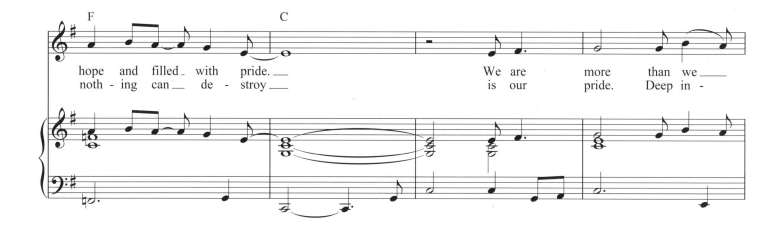

hope and filled with pride.___ We are more than we___
noth - ing can___ de - stroy___ is our pride. Deep in -

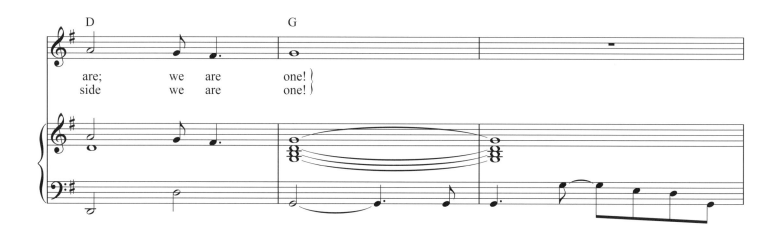

are; we are one! }
side we are one! }

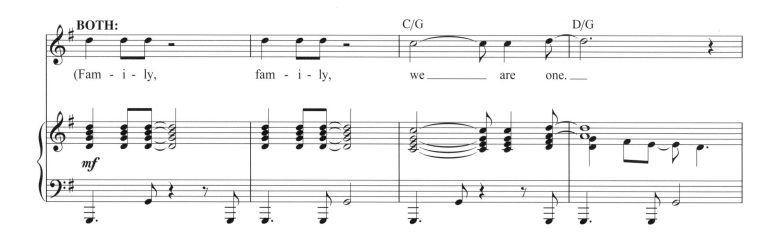

BOTH:

(Fam - i - ly, fam - i - ly, we___ are one.___

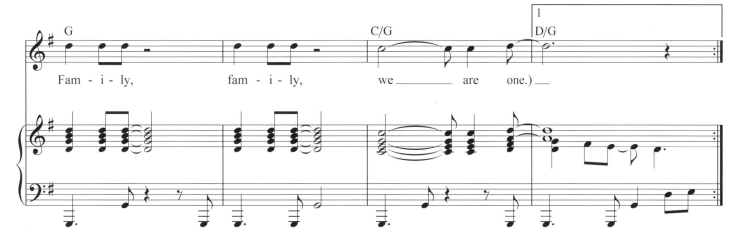

Fam - i - ly, fam - i - ly, we ___ are one.) ___

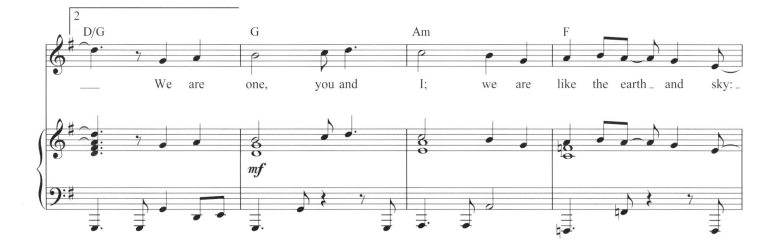

___ We are one, you and I; we are like the earth ___ and sky: ___

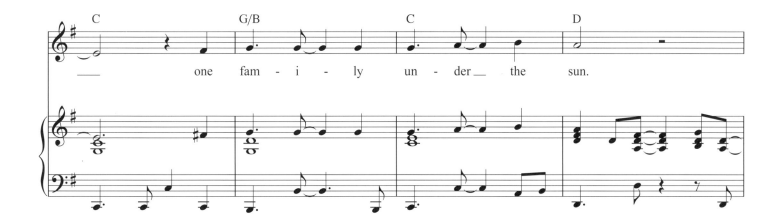

___ one fam - i - ly un - der ___ the sun.

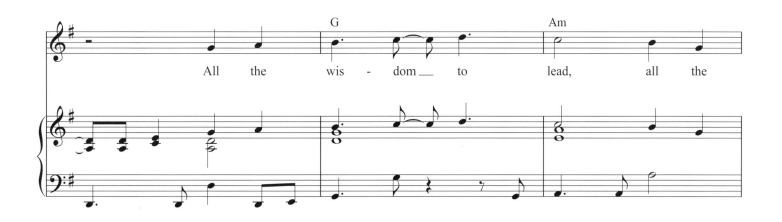

All the wis - dom ___ to lead, all the

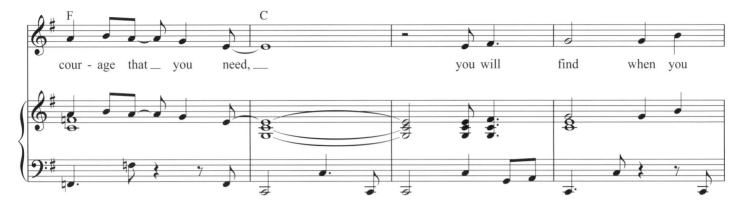

cour - age that __ you need, __ you will find when you

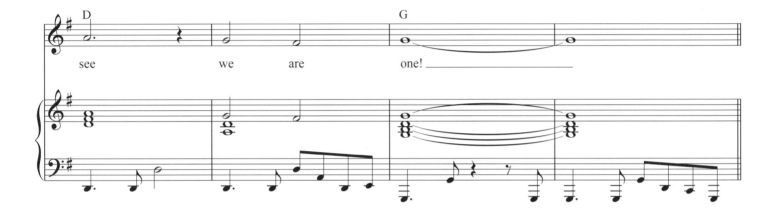

see we are one! _____

Repeat ad lib.

(Fam - i - ly, fam - i - ly, we ____ are one.) __

Play 3 times

A WHOLE NEW WORLD
from Walt Disney's *Aladdin*

Music by ALAN MENKEN
Lyrics by TIM RICE

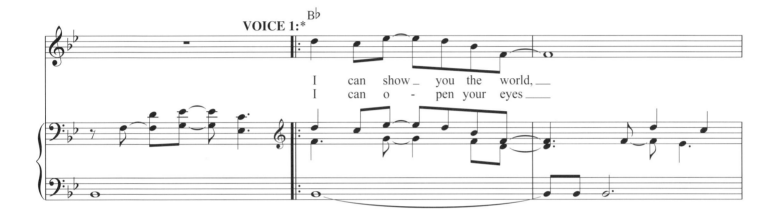

I can show you the world,
I can o-pen your eyes

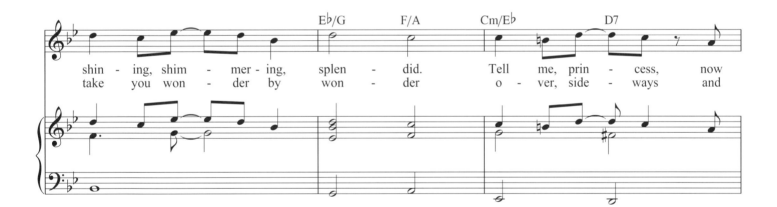

shin-ing, shim-mer-ing, splen-did. Tell me, prin-cess, now
take you won-der by won-der o-ver, side-ways and

when did you last let your heart de-cide?
un-der on a

*A duet for Aladdin and Jasmine in the film.

mag - ic car - pet ride.___ A whole new ___ world _____

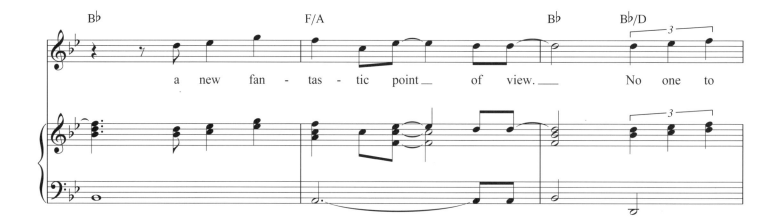

a new fan - tas - tic point ___ of view. ___ No one to

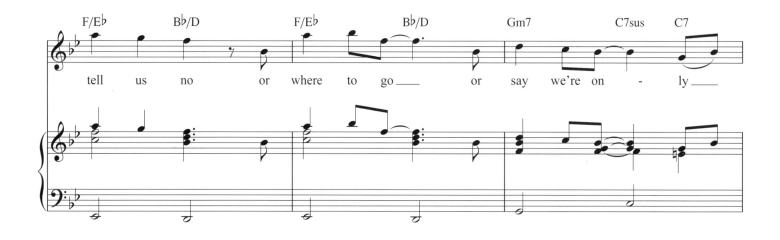

tell us no or where to go ___ or say we're on - ly ___

VOICE 2:

dream - ing. A whole new world a daz - zling

place I nev - er knew. ___ But now from way up here ___ it's

crys - tal clear ___ that now I'm in ___ a whole ___ new world ___ with

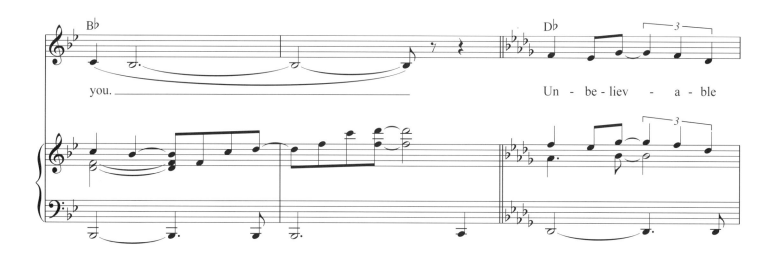

you. ___ Un - be - liev - a - ble

sights ___ in - de - scrib - a - ble feel - ing.

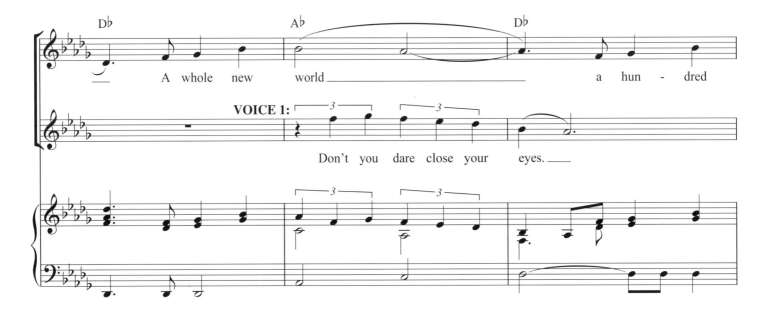

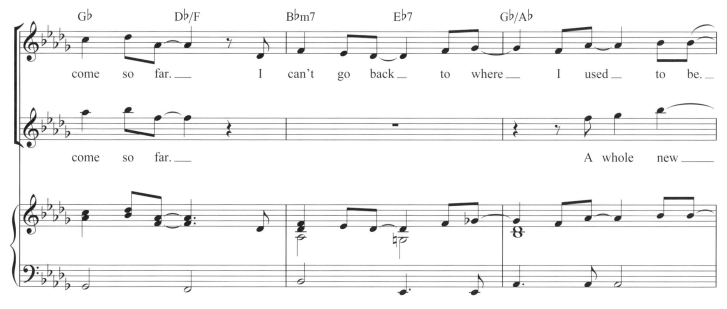

come so far. ___ I can't go back ___ to where ___ I used ___ to be. ___

come so far. ___ A whole new _____

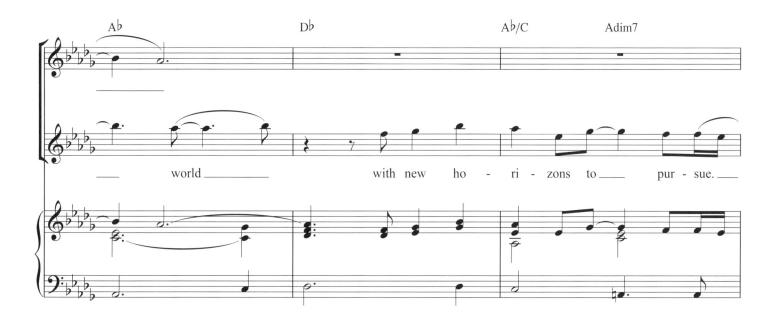

___ world _____ with new ho - ri - zons to ___ pur - sue. ___

I'll chase them an - y - where. There's time to spare.

___ I'll chase them an - y - where. There's time to spare.

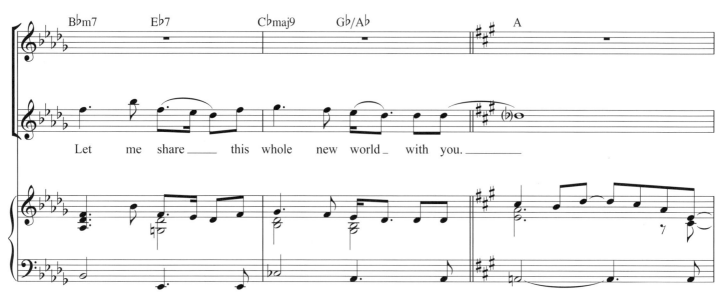

Let me share_____ this whole new world_ with you._____

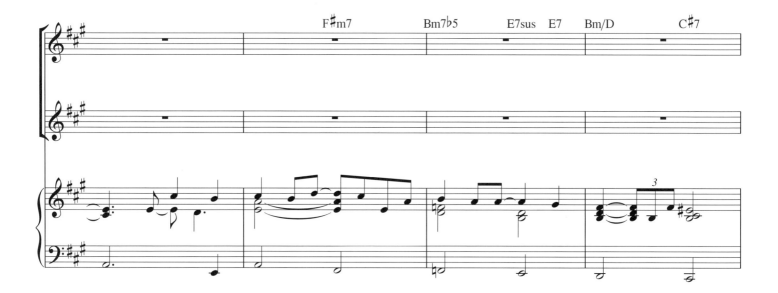

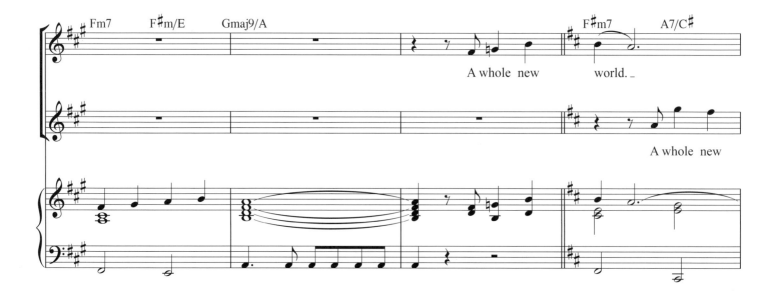

A whole new world. _

A whole new

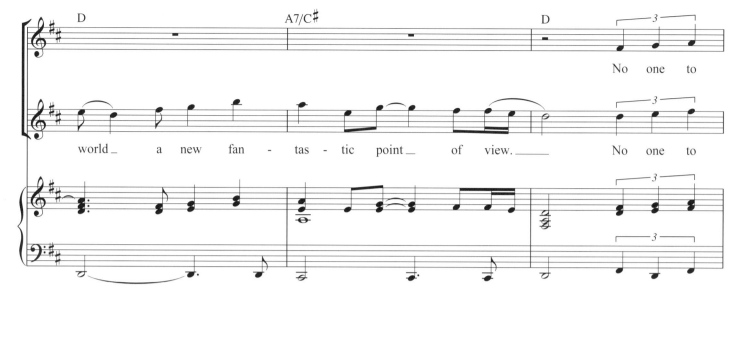

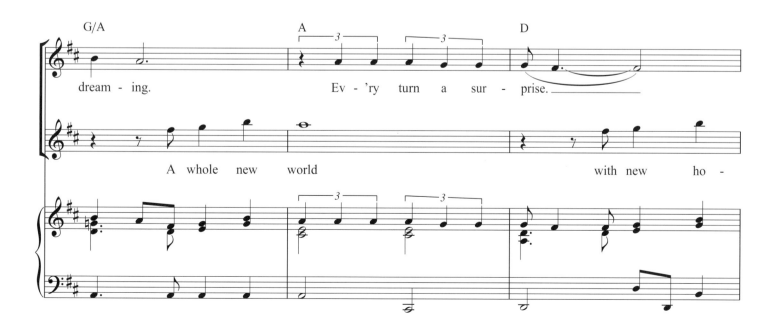

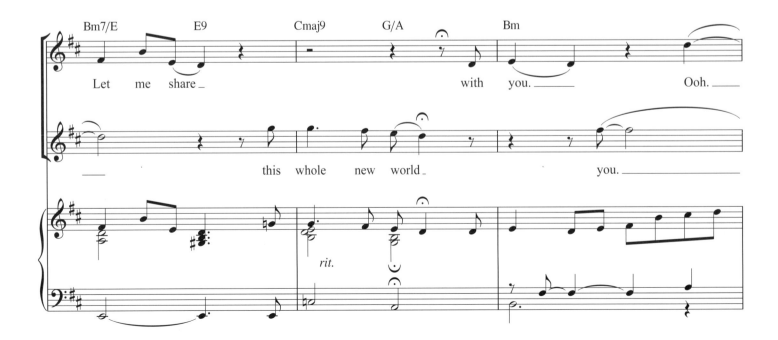

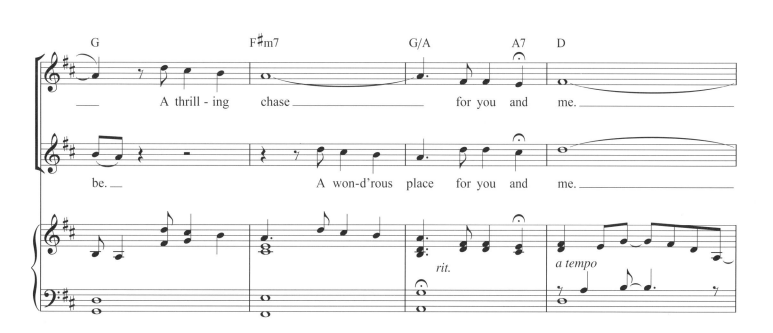

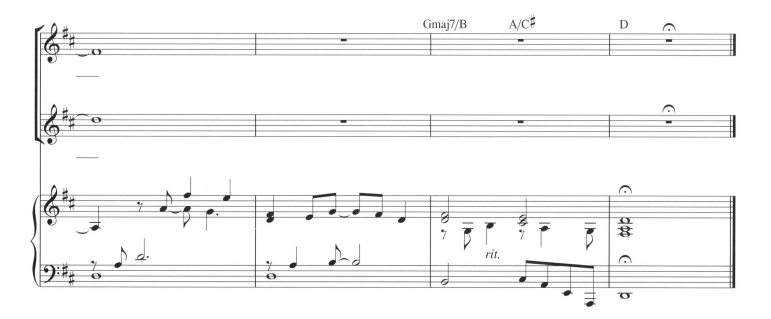